simply revland

simply revland

AN AUTOBIOGRAPHY

steven mark revland

HOW TO SUCCEED IN LIFE DESPITE YOURSELF

Charleston, SC
www.PalmettoPublishing.com

Simply Revland: How to Succeed in Life Despite Yourself

Copyright © 2022 by Steven Mark Revland

First Edition

Paperback ISBN: 979-8-8229-0936-6
eBook ISBN: 979-8-8229-0937-3

Contents

Foreword
by author Michael Morrissey

I consider it a privilege to have been invited to write the foreword to Steve Revland's magnum opus, "Simply Revland". Steve and I would first meet in late August 1965, as he, along with some of his buddies from Jefferson Elementary School filed into my seventh-grade English classroom at Agassiz Middle School. They would take seats together over by the windows and begin to prepare their defenses for whatever trouble I was likely to foist upon their lives. Steve and I were on different wavelengths at that time. He was determined to absorb as little as possible of classroom material, and I was determined that no child would leave my classroom without understanding how to diagram a sentence, and I dare say, memorize the list of prepositions in the text, in case a stranger on the street would ever need help with a prepositional phrase. Unfortunately, we were both headed on questionable journeys.

Some forty-eight years later, in 2013, my wife Susan, an artist of some repute, announced over dinner that she would be teaming up with some Fargo artists in a new gallery being constructed on Broadway in Fargo by one Steve Revland. A few weeks later she was determined to introduce me to the craftsman behind this majestic new space. We met at the doorway of his newly constructed gallery space and were about to shake hands when he blurted out, "Oh my God, it's Mr. Morrissey! It was then that I was able to reclaim an image of the young, blonde lad who sat quietly by the windows in seventh grade, thinking thoughts about the undoable and yet-to-be-done. It was an amazing, almost surreal opportunity to reestablish a relationship that had not been memorable for either of us the first time around. And that fault lies entirely with me; to steal from Shakespeare, "it has nothing to do with Brutus, or the stars!

Steve's telling of growing up in Fargo is a spellbinding adventure inside the mind of a youngster who did not learn in traditional ways. He tells of his antics as a pre-teenager, (his tree-houses, his golf courses, his singing gigs on WDAY, his short career as a grave-digger) and then his maturation into manhood. As he learned the craft of designing and creating high-end furniture virtually on his own, he became one of the most creative and vibrant voices for art in the Fargo Moorhead community.

"Simply Revland" is riveting with attendant highs and lows that one experiences in life, but it is Steve's magical way of expressing himself that makes the tale worth reading. To say that his sense of humor is unique doesn't do it justice. The reader will gain insights into the creative process and will come to know on a personal level a truly dynamic and creative man. The city of Fargo and it's surrounds owe "Rev" a deep debt of gratitude for the presence of Fine Art in the heart of the community for the last 30 years. And if you've never been to Dakota Fine Art you've now got one more thing on your bucket list.

Cletis and Edna would be bursting their buttons with the publication of this wonderful piece of memoir. Well done Steve, I am lucky to be able to call you my friend.

Preface

In January, 2021, I announced that after a fifty year career as an artist / craftsman, I would be scaling back a tish as I approach my 70's. Artists never actually retire, they just gradually and eventually tip over.....like a majestic multi-limbed tree, to put it in general terms.

Well....a year has passed and with a great deal of reflective anticipation, I feel it's time to tell my story. It's no secret to many that as I approach my 70th trip around the sun.....I have yet to read an actual book. "How is this" you may ask? This will all be explained as you weave your way through this autobiography, titled "simply revland". The publisher stated that I may be the first author to have written a book before actually consuming one. What a novel experiment, (no pun intended).

I certainly hope you will enjoy my book, and perhaps even glean something from it. For everyone else.....forgive me for being so overbearingly presumptuous. I can't help myself.

Introduction

Welcome to "simply revland", a collection of memories and musings spanning eight decades as an artist and musician, most notably the last fifty years as an award winning designer and furniture maker. Like my sister, mother, and grandmother before me, I have been a notorious note taker, which has served me well, as I now have a treasure trove of stories to tell, unsolicited advice to give, and quite possibly, admissions to dole out.

I'd like to thank a specific therapist, who told me very early on in life:

"As I've gotten to know and understand you....you may find it advantageous to record and write things down, for if you don't, you might forget those very things that bring you value. You may also want to schedule your day on paper, and cross out tasks as you achieve them. Otherwise.... the walls that you continue to bounce off of might just imprison you."

Very wise advice given to an ADHD afflicted man-child in his early twenties, trying to find his way in a highly competitive baby boomer world, with barely a high school diploma in his back pocket.

I write these chapters, past and present.....hoping to leave some form of legacy for my son, a chip off the old block, and quite possibly for myself, for as I continue along this glorious path, I may need to read about myself to remember who I was. Such would be life. Enjoy!

CHAPTER ONE

The Early Years

1955

Ah yes....the 1950's. For those who had the pleasure or opportunity to grow up during that period, I'm sure you can relate. Life was simple and things moved at a much slower pace. Without advanced technology, computers, internet, cell phones, and a 24 hour a day news cycle, we had more of a tendency to live in the moment.....not remotely aware of what the future held for us.

As much as I'd like to remember symbolically picking up this piece of wood as a two year old in 1955, my earliest authentic memory as a child was my first day of kindergarten in 1958. Jefferson municipal elementary grade school was tucked away in a cozy blue collar neighborhood, a middle class community where most folks struggled to make ends meet. My parents worked extremely hard to provide for the four of us kids. We didn't ask for much knowing that....plus we had nothing to compare our lives with. We were content. We survived on home cooked meals and hand me down clothing, and Friday nights were reserved for homemade pizza as we gathered around the backyard fire pit listening to my Dad, Cletis, play tunes on his harmonica. Oh my.

My first day of kindergarten was also my sister Catherine's first day as a journalism student at the University of North Dakota in Grand Forks. I missed her desperately, as she certainly wouldn't have allowed me to wear a Bat Masterson outfit to school the entire month of September. I guess I thought I was pretty cool.....even though my older brother Paul wouldn't properly admit we were in any way related.

Evenings and weekends were spent canvassing my parents 50 by 150 plot of land that our house was centered on, and what I could do with this land, (with my parents permission of course.) I soon realized I was a dreamer.....as this was how my brain worked, and it didn't take me long to understand that the educational curriculum required for schooling wasn't readily available for me, for whatever I was attempting to read was not being absorbed and/or registering in my head. It didn't seem to bother me.....as I had other plans....big plans.

CHAPTER TWO

The Magical Mystery Door

1960

N ever tell this to a 7 year old. "Do not open that door on the side of the porch". This drove me crazy. I knew there was something mysterious about its contents. Hinges on the top of the door? And no lock on it? Kinda weird if you were to ask a child. What if I got trapped inside there, I thought. Does Dad have a flashlight? Are there raccoons holed up inside? Spiders? Or worse yet....a band of Jehovah's Witnesses abandoning their door to door modus operandi? Seeing as I was growing up in a Christian atmosphere, I couldn't use the word "hell"......
so I thought....what the "heck's" under that porch anyway. Even my thoughts required purity. I probably walked by that door 1000 times before I got up the nerve to take a peek.

Turns out even a peek requires some level of admonishment. I always knew I was in trouble when Cletis and Edna would speak to each other in Norwegian. I eventually did learn that "vi har skjemt bort ham" meant "I think we have spoiled him".

During that peek under the porch......I noticed a lot of material..... stacked to the hilt, in a total disarray. I made an agreement with Cletis that I would organize the items in exchange for an obvious "better look" at what was there. He agreed.

Like many of my 2nd grade classmates, I was a latchkey kid..... meaning both parents needed to work to get by, allowing a modicum of unsupervised freedom between 3 and 5 o'clock. This was a perfect time to gradually pick away at the under-the-porch contents. Anoth-

er benefit derived from being a latchkey kid was, as studies have shown, the child retains a profound state of person-al independence. That being said....I viewed this attribute as a blessing, because.....quite frankly, I had things to do.

I desperately despised school....considering it a waste of time. If there was a class called "hooky", I would have aced that lying down. Eventu-ally, Jefferson's principal, Glenn Melvey, came to our home and chased me around the back-yard, hoping to apprehend

Teri Bach, my girlfriend, therapist, and backyard architectural consultant

me....which to his credit, he eventually did. Fortunately, Mr Melvey was not well versed in Norwegian.

Back to the "Magical Mystery Door". The opening, on the east side of the house, (consequential morning sun) led to 250 square feet of "Alice in Wonderland" for me, and probably only me.....with my skull thoroughly full of mush. Its contents provided me with everything I needed to paint my canvas.....which was my backyard, my solace, and security blanket. I was a child with a dream, with big plans, as well as time on his hands. Hands that eventually, and subsequently would be my instruments of joy, as well as success in life.

CHAPTER THREE

The Fort

1961

According to Webster…..a fort is a place that's made strong and secure. It can also be a fortress or a fortification. But for a child….. it can simply be a patchwork quilt held up by clothespins or a large cardboard box turned upside down. Simplicity…..as an 8 year old, seems like the most logical route toward a satisfactory outcome, unless you have a treasure trove of raw material beneath the front porch, permission to use it, and a blueprint leading toward a continuation of solitude and independence. I was beside myself. Literally. A potential clubhouse for one.

I had no pretentious visions of grandeur, or intention of creating some sort of Taj Mahal. I had yet to develop the required skills. I was, however, able to imagine that I did….a somewhat ridiculous notion for sure. But…..that imagination is one skill that seemed to arrive just when it was needed, along with a hammer, hand saw, some used nails, and a plethora of

2 by 4's, plywood, used siding and shingles, all waiting for me behind the magical mystery door.

As long as I was able to slap up 4 walls and a pitched roof…..I was good to go, until my vision of a pot belly stove, complete with a chimney, entered my imaginary architectural blueprint. Winter was approaching and if I didn't want to envision "hooky" as a seasonal sport, this source of heat was imperative.

Now…..when I think of my parents, Cletis and Edna, I'm reminded of the long running "Peanuts" comic strip series. Ageless children, Charlie Brown, Linus, Pigpen, and Lucy….somehow living in a fantasy world void of adult chaperones. No parents….no supervision. What a beautiful premise it is and was…..as it was perfectly indicative of my life experience outside the home. How could they not reign me in. I mean really. Installing a crude wood burning stove in a backyard fort as an 8 year old? Seriously? Perhaps they knew something I wasn't aware of. Perhaps they saw me as a special needs child, someone who potentially required additional skills of self preservation. I never asked them.

The Revland "clubhouse" was a huge success, for me anyway. I eventually allowed my best friend "Beaver" to join. He lived down the block on 3rd Avenue and was a legendary character. That being said…..he understood me. One day we had a good laugh over the shack's lack of an escalator, something he and I worshiped at the downtown Woolworths Store on Broadway.

In closing….the clubhouse was a fortuitous prelude to each

backyard project to follow…..a stepping stone toward developing the skill sets required for future success. I had more plans, and an abundance of imagination in my tool box.

Chapter Four

The Treehouse

1962

'll never forget the view as I sat comfortably in the penthouse, or the "crows nest", as I so proudly called it. It was the third level of my treehouse, my private bachelor pad. Measuring 30 feet off the ground.... it was my official den of iniquity. Musty old pillows stuffed into an old burlap potato sack, neatly and precisely nestled into one of the remaining tree crotches, made for a comfortable place for my backside. I proceeded to rustle up a rich supply of Readers Digests, and sufficiently crammed them into a shelf unit strapped to a corresponding tree branch. It was impressive. The reading material was undoubtedly a distraction, I guess only there to impress others.....the others that unfortunately never came, due to the fear factor attached to the skill level required to reach this high level of achievement. I never realized that 30 feet might seem like 50 to a fellow 9 year old classmate. A fearless monkey I was.

The middle level required more material from under the porch, which oddly seemed to replenish itself as I used it, I naively surmised. Being 9 had its delusional benefits. However....I guess I was smart enough to avoid nailing boards into the tree, this 100 year old towering gray Elm straddling the property line between us and the Gustafsons. So I used a lot of rope, which I also found under the porch, and cut the wood to precisely fit between the limbs. I learned how to tie a square knot in the Cub Scouts, which really came in handy. This middle level was my living room, my parlor, proving much easier to access by my friend Beaver, and served as a congenial space for us to discuss politics.

The lowest level of the treehouse was my bedroom......my pride and joy. About 12 feet off the ground, easily the coziest spot in the tree. I spent a lot of time designing this space, knowing I would actually be sleeping there when the folks weren't aware of it. It turns out that this was no secret to Cletis and Edna, as they once again continued to supply me with an abundance of freedom and independence. I later discovered that this freedom was mine, I had earned it, and it appeared the other children on the block weren't as deserving. When you are a loner.....you inherit a wandering mind.

Oh how I wish Cletis had taken photographs of my treehouse, and perhaps he did. But I guess one must at times use their imagination to recall specific memories from years ago. Think of this story as a piece of fiction, even though it's very much real. Picture yourself in the crows nest. Try and feel the cool breeze as it brushes against your face and whistles by your ears, ruffling your hair. Crack a smile and remain as still as possible, as a tiny sparrow lands just feet from your face, oblivious that small human beings can actually invade their territory without startling them.

Experience the tree swaying back and forth in the breeze, causing a bit of unease, as you make your way down to the lower level bedroom. Lay yourself down in that bed…..and gleefully peer through the leaves at the flowering crab next door. Imagine that no one is aware that you even exist, as this is actually what appealed to me at the time. I was a certified, bonafide loner, but had good reason to be. Stay tuned….

Chapter Five

Solitude

The Early Years

Six times four equals......."twenty-four!" I would blurt out. Eighteen divided by two equals........."nine!" I would claim with confidence. Flash cards can be a useful tool in preparing a young child for the 1st grade. I vaguely recall enjoying these learning sessions I had with my older sisters, but at the same time.....wondered if they had something better to do, being 10 and 12 years older. Perhaps they knew something about me that I didn't know.....and felt a need to provide me with some additional guidance. My three older siblings all were quite accomplished scholastically, but my potential at achieving that elevated status was a certified crap shoot. I was the proverbial black sheep of the family.

My first two years of grade school I received straight A's, primarily because my sisters, through the use of flash cards and spelling bee's, sent a subliminal message to the teaching staff and administrators that this child was gifted. I recall meeting with principal Melvey and my mother Edna about the school's plans to move me ahead 2 grades for English and Math, which meant walking down the hall for those two classes, where normally you would stay in the same classroom all day. This arrangement would eventually fail miserably …and bring me down emotionally.

My sister's intent, bless their hearts…..was to give me a head start. Those intentions were pure as gold. But as soon as what I had initially memorized fell short of acquiring new information through studious reading……I was unfortunately lost. There is a reason I have yet to read a book at the age of 69. I have lived with ADHD and dyslexia all of my life. I would love to be able to put a humorous spin on this chapter, but I can't, so therefore I won't. But the information provided herein…..will help the audience understand the premise of the book.

This is where it gets worse, and you may want to move the children to another room. Due to the pressure to function and succeed as a student, I started to develop facial tics. Eyes blinking, neck stretching, head shaking…..and eventually, owl type noises emerging from my voice box. I was a freak….and fellow classmates let me know about it. Learning was impossible for me….and the only way to lessen the ticks? Isolation and putting an end to the process of learning the traditional way. The ticks continued until my freshman year in high school, and the bullies had no mercy. Tourette's syndrome was not only humiliating…..it was exhausting, and took a lot of energy to keep it at bay.

There is no reason to provide more detail about this portion of my life, only that it was a necessary evil…..loaning me the tools to shape my life as an artist and musician. It was what it was…..and I know I'm not alone.

In closing….I realize that this chapter may appear out of sync…… but I wasn't quite sure where to place it. Hence…. the story of my life. However…..there was always hope, so let's move on to more positive adventures. Stay tuned.

CHAPTER SIX

Party Line

1963

S pring was in the air in 1963. I was perfectly cognizant that there were only a couple months remaining before summer break, and that 4th grade was soon to be known as an in-the-rear-view-mirror afterthought. It was also an oddly rare occasion that I was ever allowed to leave class early at Jefferson Grade School, in view of my reputation for actually failing to show up. I had my eye on the clock all day, knowing I had permission to leave at 1:30. Why? Because I was heading downtown.

In the early 60's, downtown was the heartbeat of Fargo. It was where the action was. All of it. Especially since at the time, it was geographically and conveniently centered in the city. Fargo had grown somewhat equally, north and south of Main Avenue, and the term "mall" hadn't invaded our vocabulary quite yet. No strip malls, no West Acres, no Northport. Downtown was the home to JC Penney, Sears, Woolworths, Straus Clothiers, Leeby's Deli, numerous movie theaters, along with an abundance of pubs and restaurants. The economy was exemplary, and the hustle and bustle was copiously contagious. Another Downtown landmark was at 207 5th Street North, the home of WDAY TV, which just so happened to be my mid-afternoon destination. I had an engagement to perform on the variety show "Party Line" with my 19 year old sister Claudia, who a few months earlier had been crowned Miss Fargo. Oh my.

I remember getting my first guitar from Claudia when I was about 6. It was quite large for my body, as my tiny frame was probably more suited for a ukulele. But I made it work. Learning just a few basic chords meant adding a number of songs to our repertoire. G, C, and D7 were an easy learn, but the necessary F chord was a stretch for my tiny fingers. She and I had been rehearsing for weeks for this television appearance, perfecting a Norwegian folk song, Andy Williams's "Moon River" and a few other classics from The Kingston Trio and newly formed Peter Paul and Mary.

Verna Newell, a local celebrity, hosted "Party Line," this long-running afternoon variety show on WDAY, from 1957 to 1979, and secured guests like Gregory Peck, Lawrence Welk, Dustin Hoffman, and even the likes of "Tiny Tim" in the early 70's. The notion of performing on TV a whole decade before Tiny Tim was pretty hard to fathom, but a badge I'm happy to wear. Verna had a number of guest host sidekicks, like the legendary Bill Weaver and Boyd Christianson, both doing their best Ed McMahon renditions.

Now let's get this straight. My dear sister was extremely talented, and quite capable of pulling this off without me. To this day....I can't understand why she thought it was a good idea to join her as I was more than capable of really screwing this up, between potential stage fright, facial tics, and just being a 9 year old. But we pulled it off..... harmonies and all. The next year Claudia became Miss North Dakota and was in the Miss America Pageant in 1964. She soon will turn 80 and is as beautiful as ever. Throughout the entire decade of the 60's,

Verna kept asking me back to perform as a solo act......which only cemented in my mind that she had developed a serious crush on me.

The Moral to this story? Understanding that this handshake thing at WDAY that adults performed with each other appeared to be some sort of ritual, perhaps cult-like, and that those in charge will even reach out their hand to a 9 year old child as long as you freely accommodate them. I  also learned that a good solid squeeze was what these adults at WDAY yearned for, so I eventually obliged them, which oddly seemed to be fodder for a good old belly laugh. Secondly.....the way to work your way around symptoms of Tourette's Syndrome was to sing and play guitar on TV. If only I could have done this every day. Stay tuned.....

CHAPTER SEVEN

The Wood Lathe

1965

My first thought was that he was a smoker. His huge, gray, over-grown nicotine-stained mustache hung over his top lip, weakening his smile.....if there ever was one. He talked infrequently in a gruff voice as he shuffled awkwardly across the dusty floor. Most noticeably however, was the shocking realization that half of his fingers were gone. As in, missing. For a 12 year old, it was initially quite confusing and a bit intimidating. I certainly was intrigued. But, on top of everything else, I was on pins and needles. You see.....this was my first day of 7th grade woodshop class at Agassiz Junior High School. New classmates, new teachers, new location, and an influx of bullies. Home was now 5 blocks away....a much longer distance to be chased by those feeling a need to torment me. Regardless, expectations at this new school were much higher. Mr Engh was my woodshop instructor and this could obviously take some getting used to.

My brother (Paul) had Mr. Engh four years earlier, and tales circulating about him had reached folklore status: Like the day he lobbed off one of his fingers on the bandsaw, threw it in the waste basket, crudely applied a bandage, and went about his day like nothing happened. He obviously was a tough old bird, a man's man, with perhaps some personal issues or a pre-existing condition. Regardless.....as I got to know this lovely man, his shop became my escape route….my refuge. While most kids were watching the clock for the bell to ring, I was wishing that the hands on my personal timepiece would slow to a crawl. This space was like home to me…..and I needed a home away from home.

One thing I learned early on: We were too young and immature to operate the power tools, which I found quite condescending. We were relegated to hand planing boards and gluing them together for cutting boards. I was quite bored, as I should be, for someone who had already built an outdoor fort, complete with a pot belly stove, and a three-level tree house. I also thought I should have my own car….but rules are rules, I assume. I guess it's imperative that one can see over the steering wheel.

It wasn't until Mr Engh demonstrated the act of turning a spindle on the wood lathe that my whistle was thoroughly moisturized. Quite frankly, the lathe was probably the most dangerous power tool in the shop, and could lob off a finger in a heartbeat, which made me wonder if Mr Engh had spent a little too much time at the lathe. All I knew was this: I had to have one. Yes. I had to have one. However, again, therein lies the rub. First of all, we were poor, and the folks weren't in a position to dole out the funds for purchasing one. Secondly, if they had any idea how remarkably dangerous this power tool was, they undoubtedly wouldn't allow it in the house. Or would they? Up to now, Cletis and Edna had drawn a fine line between what was dangerous (or potentially harmful), and what could continue to provide me with independence and a higher level of self esteem.

All told, not withstanding every circumstance, I was forced to create my own home spun wood lathe. Yes.....I was only 12 years old, and it probably wasn't in any prepubescent playbook. But I was a stubborn young lad and I eagerly processed fulfillment. The most critical find was an old Maytag washing machine motor, neatly tucked away under the basement stairway. No doubt a Cletis "treasure" until now. This motor, in woodworking terms, was the potential "livestock", generally speaking, and what made the world go 'round.....at a very high speed. Most wood lathes had a variable speed component to them, but this one would be classified at, what I thought at the time, a "million" RPM's, quite suitable for turning wood stock, if not also capable of causing a fly-by-the-seat-of-my-pants premature death in the family. Cletis and Edna spent the majority of their time upstairs, so they were fortunately oblivious to the commotion going on in the dungeon.....which was a blessing.

After drilling 2 holes in the motor's pulley, I securely tapped 2 six-penny nails into the pulley, making the livestock complete. After bolting the motor to the workbench, I rounded up an old Douglas Fir 4 by 4 from under the porch, which would serve as my "tail stock". I ground an old half inch bolt to a point using Grandpa Revland's hand grinder, and tapped it into the 4 by 4, completing my tail stock. I then hand hewed some scrap iron on Grandpa's grinder, fashioning some skews for shaping the wood as it spun on the lathe. After wiring the plug on the motor I was ready to plug it in. Yes. Uh huh.

Yes….it is one thing to make a potentially dangerous machine as a 12 year old, it's another thing to actually plug it in. So after gluing two oak boards together to make it square, I securely attached this future inaugural spindle into place and plugged in the motor. As I quickly backed away, it was then that I wondered……have I gone too far this time? Is this crazy ass speed and sound of this twirling piece of wood worth the risk? I wish I could recall exactly….but I think I took a time out to give this some serious thought….or examine my interpretation of creativity, or bravery for that matter. Eventually, bravery won out and the result was more gratifying than I ever imagined, and the satisfaction was delightfully palatable. Up to now….the adventure leading up to and surrounding the creation of this oak spindle was my greatest achievement, and something I have had on my shelf for 57 years. (See photo)

CHAPTER EIGHT

The Revland Municipal

1967

U sing a freshly sharpened serrated bread knife, I positioned the oversized empty soup can on the neatly trimmed grass. Using the can to guide the knife into the soil, I created the perfect fit for the can itself. After removing the mixture of clay and topsoil, I repeated this process in six unique locations within the confines of the backyard. It was the final procedural necessity before unveiling my latest project to the neighborhood peeps. I had already developed a reputation for my quirky yearly projects....and I'm quite confident most Jefferson parents assume I'm primarily an attention getter.

Contrary to popular belief....these projects actually began as therapy to ward off the effects of my Tourette's affliction, and ended up being a tool to make friends. This physical abnormality was gradually on the wane, and I felt the need to make up for lost time, socially. A fort, complete with a wood stove, a multilevel treehouse, multiple yearly toboggan slides, a football field complete with goal posts and night lights, a high jumping pit, and last but not least, a pole vaulting pit, which became a much needed practice area if I was to make the track team as a freshman.

My last hurrah....and perhaps the most complex, was to create the Revland Municipal Golf Course on our family property, as I couldn't Imagine a better way to make friends in the neighborhood and beyond. Providing the  "gentleman's game", one of history's oldest and most revered sports, with free admission, was a decision I would not regret, as high school was beginning in the Fall. Junior High was in the books, as a distant wasted memory. I despised it, and I'm sure to this day, is why I have very little memory of it. The golf course was a few years in the making, so to make it as authentic as possible within a 50 by 150 foot lot, I needed to use my imagination, which was always available in my toolbox, and obviously much needed at this time.

A few years earlier, in the Parade insert in the Fargo Forum, I saw an ever-repeating ad for Bermuda Creeping Bentgrass, a breed of grass used for putting greens on golf courses. It was drought resistant, winter hardy, and most important, (trying my best to hold back laughter) going to be "over seeded" in Cletis and Edna's backyard, in logistically located areas. I can't believe my parents allowed me to do this, but after a couple years of growth, it overtook the Kentucky Bluegrass that had existed before, and the push mower could be lowered to about a quarter inch, allowing the golf ball to roll at about 6 on the stimpmeter (which measured speed on the green). I ended up with 6 amoeba shaped greens, 3 of which were used twice, to give me a 9 hole golf course.

I once heard my parents tell some family friends: "First you raise children.....then you raise grass"

Obviously, on paper, I had already designed the course, the tee boxes, and even a potential "back nine" option, which I eventually utilized, giving even more variety to the landscape. The key now to the equation, was the "ball", and how to still utilize a "full swing"..... having the ability to shape the ball around a dog leg. For those of you who aren't golfers, I'm really sorry. I probably lost you a paragraph ago. To those who are, this chapter could act as a recipe for a lake home 3 holer, which I guess would require some maintenance, so enter at your own risk.

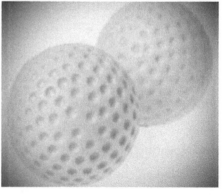

So.....the ball. There are two types of plastic balls: a wiffle ball, with holes in it, and a hollow solid ball, which goes three times as far, and can be curved according to how you swing the club. This memory is creating more salivating on my end, as I would trade my current set of clubs to go back for just a day.

Nostalgia set aside…the hollow, solid plastic ball was the cat's meow. The first tee was in the front yard and required a moonshot over the house to a corner-of-the-yard slightly sloped green….a par 4. Once you are on the green, you replace the plastic ball with a real one, and attempt to roll it into the Campbell's soup can. I fondly recall the sound the ball made as it dropped in the hole. Clank! Priceless.

Brother Paul

In closing…..the Revland Municipal was a huge hit in the neighborhood, and introduced the great game of golf to a number of my new friends. As far as the scorecards? My brother Paul graduated from Central High School that Spring, providing me with hundreds of unused graduation pictures. Much to his chagrin, I typed up the course information on the backside of his mugshot. I mistakenly assumed he would be honored to have the course named after him. He didn't see it that way.

CHAPTER NINE

Slowpitch Softball

1968

I wasn't alone.....sitting patiently on the sloping hillside. My good friends, Willy and Knute, were also in attendance that day, flanked on each side of me, exuding the same mutual apprehension as fans of all ages gathered at the Mickelson NorthSide Softball Complex, diamond number 2. It was the summer of 1968 and we were forced to sit on the grassy knoll that day, only because the aluminum bleachers were fully occupied. Excitement was in the air.....and you could cut it with a knife as we waited for the home team to take the field. We were about to become witnesses to a new sport being introduced to the Fargo community. A sport that would change, alter, and enhance my life for more than 40 years.

The three of us were on the edge of our grass stained numbed backsides as we observed the "Air National Guard Mustangs" take the field for pregame warmups. The agra-lime infield had been meticulously raked and the over-seeded lush outfield grass appeared to have been mowed by a professional, as it had the appearance of suede on an expensive winter coat. This was a really big deal, as it should have been.

Life was very simple in 1968. We didn't have much else to do, or look forward to for that matter. Our ticket for today was punched. We were immensely and essentially preoccupied, as today we were witnessing history, albeit an exhibition game, appropriately called "Slowpitch Softball."

I peered over at Willy as we observed the first warmup pitch. The red-stitched, blue-dot ball was artfully lofted into the air, with at least a 10 foot arch. We then watched it plop down a few inches behind the diamond shaped home plate. Thud. It was a thing of beauty. The three of us were mesmerized, and even a bit perplexed, as we all were veterans of peewee and midget baseball growing up, and were accustomed to battling a fast ball or an occasional curveball, some of us with limited success.

I, for one, struggled in peewee baseball. It seemed like I either struck out, walked, or was unfortunately hit by a pitch. I don't recall ever hitting it out of the infield, which was rather demeaning. Before today, my future with the red stitched hard ball was limited.....until now. This new game of Slowpitch softball was tailor made for me. Manna from Heaven.

In the summer of 1969, the Fargo Moorhead Slowpitch Association was established, consisting of only four teams. Fastpitch softball was still "king," as it had been for decades, and had a tendency to attract the local "athletes". We soon discovered that if you played Slowpitch, you were considered a pansy, or a chump. But to put things into perspective..... fast forwarding 50 years, there are now at least 1000 Slowpitch teams in the state, with fewer than 30 Fastpitch teams. It appears the "athletes" found another game to play. All this being said.....we were pioneers in 1969, and I was proud to be one of them, even though, at the time, I was considered a chump. I got over it.

The sponsor of one of those initial 4 teams was Wimmers Jewelry. Brad Wimmer had a reputation for acquiring great talent, and we soon began a softball dynasty as one of the top softball teams in the state for 17 years. As the game of Slowpitch quickly, and exponentially expanded year to year, we also developed a repu-tation. I never considered myself to be an intimidating figure, but we, as a team, decided that we were in a position to use that tac-tic as a continued key to our suc-cess. We were young, wearing white spikes and snazzy double  knit uniforms. We bore long hair, ear piercings, had blazing speed, great defense, and a team-wide menacing scowl that we utilized with great af-fection against our competition. No trash talking, just a continual stare down, with the scowl conveniently attached.

Most of us had frightening nicknames as well, that we used to our advantage:

- Rev (the Reverend) Revland
- Mark (the Mortician) Moret
- Tom (Hannibal Lecter) Lechner
- Willy (Give me the Willies) Williams

—were just a few. Yes, we were one of the best teams in the state, yet one of the most hated as well. We admittedly were a bit on the cocky side. If you need proof, look at the picture (next page) after one of our many weekend tournament victories. Do you see any smiles on these faces? Only the late great Arnie (the Joker) Opp (bottom row, left end) seemed happy about winning that day. Me, (top row, second from right), seemed content in showing no emotion with the rest of my fellow hooligans. We were an enigma. Mysterious. It is what made us great!

In closing......If I had the time or space, I could spin hundreds of great softball stories that occurred over 5 decades, so I will spare you. What I can tell you is this. I played on only two teams over a 37 year period. Wimmers Jewelry, 17 years, (third base) and Rooters Bar, 20 years, (shortstop). My career ended in 2006 at the age of 53, due to rotator cuff surgery. In 2008, I was inducted into the North Dakota Softball Hall of Fame in Jamestown ND. They have inducted 4 players every spring since 1957, and I am so honored to be included with such legendary talent.

Before leaving for Jamestown for the induction ceremony, I was

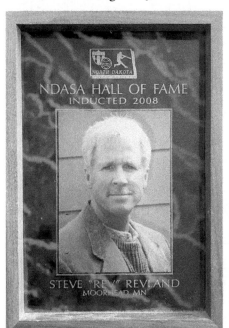

advised by my wife to leave my scowl at home, housing it in the closet with my personalized aluminum bat and old weathered leather fielding glove. As I have for years, I rely on her judgment and wisdom to guide me.

CHAPTER TEN

Senior Year

1971

It was mid-morning in the Spring of 1971. Just another typical and unremarkable Tuesday or Thursday. While our fellow students were back in class at Fargo South High School, we were combing through the ball rack at the Bowler on South University Drive, a weekly required ritual meant to track down our perfectly fit, black-colored, three-holed sphere. The bowling alley was usually empty around 10 am, so finding the same ball each visit was a simplistic task, as was selecting our choice of lane. By now…we were on a first name basis. It was a typical day.

We weren't even very good bowlers, but it really didn't matter much. We were being a bit rebellious, and there was some thrill to that I guess. By 11:30…..we were settling into our pink vinyl upholstered two seater booth at Pinky's

Pizza Parlor, next to Agassiz Junior High, for our weekly pepperoni pie, which we customarily washed down with a can of Coca Cola. We were certainly proverbial creatures of habit.

My friend (I will call him Lee) and I enjoyed these Tuesdays and Thursdays, as by now, missing class really didn't seem to matter. Neither of us was going to college, we each had Vietnam hanging over our heads, and the odds of us actually graduating with the rest of the class were slim and none. The future…..if my memory serves me well, wasn't so bright. Both Lee and I worked in the afternoon. He, at King Leo's drive-in, and I, at Dakota National Bank in Downtown Fargo. We each got a class credit for working, and crammed in our remaining required classes in the morning, most of which I never attended. I obviously wasn't your poster child for educational development, and with graduation on the horizon, Cletis and Edna were in for a rude awakening. Report cards were coming out soon and their youngest child would not be graduating. Just another family embarrassment.

The last few weeks of May was when everyone was cramming for finals, taking their college entrance exams, and for a few of us derelicts, participating in Senior "skip" day, a tradition the administration was not fond of,  understandably so. Senior "skip" day was the ultimate form of redundancy in my world, as pretty much every day was "skip" day. One thing I would not advise, however, was consuming whiskey in a van down by the river, then returning to study hall. I had spent the better part of 4 years trying not to make a fool of myself. That abruptly came to a screeching halt during the 2 o'clock hour. Trust me….these occurrences are not something I'm proud of, and hope that any parent reading this would spend an inordinate amount of time with their child emphasizing the importance of an education.

Report cards came out right before Memorial Day, appropriately so, as the confrontation with Cletis and Edna would be memorialized forever. 4 credits short, 45 absences, and a GPA of .08. I remember Edna having to take a seat to absorb what she just read. And I, at the same time, wondered how I possibly could have achieved a .08, thinking the instructors were being more than generous. After doing the math, I realized it was my "C" average I earned in Wood Shop that brought me up to such an impressive level.

Needless to say, college entrance exams or the annual graduation ceremony rehearsal was not on the menu for me.....until Edna received a phone call from my class counselor, Russ Riveland, (no relation). "Why wasn't Steve at the graduation rehearsal," Russ asked, to which Edna swiftly reminded him of my remarkable scholastic achievements and my feeble attempt to fervently graduate last in my class. "Do you really think we want him back here next year," he replied? He encouraged her to be certain that I would attend the ceremony.

It was late May, 1971, at the Fargo Civic Center. The place was packed, as being a baby boomer, it was one of the largest classes of students on record. My parents and my brother, Paul, were conveniently situated in the top row,  (or the nosebleed section), not because they arrived late, but to avoid embarrassment as I was instructed to give them a "thumbs up" or a "thumbs down," referring to the realization that I was a proud recipient of a signed high school diploma. As the MC called out my name, I felt a bit sheepish, completely undeserving, as I tried not to trip over my oversized brown and gold robe, something I was fitted for that evening.

The beauty of this moment, after 4 years of total failure, was that none of my classmates even remotely realized that I was a complete and utter derelict. Everyone was smiling, as was I, when I discovered that my diploma was signed. I quickly gave my family a "thumbs up" signal, as the medical staff tried to revive Edna.

I'm kind of surprised that this chapter was this lengthy, as high school was a total non-event for me, which might lend itself to a lack of material to write about. Again....I don't recommend or endorse this type of behavior for any young individual today, as getting an education is imperative in today's highly competitive world. These were my choices, under the circumstances, and I'm pretty sure I realized the consequences. Or did I?

In closing.....some of you might surmise that this chapter, a summary of my attempt at an education, is rather pathetic or quite sad. But I assure you, don't feel bad for me, as I actually bowled over 200 on numerous occasions.

CHAPTER ELEVEN

Grave Diggin' Blues

1972

It was an unusually wet Spring in 1972, and Grandpa Revland had just recently passed away at the age of 86. I had just returned home from a buying trip at our local Kmart in my yellow 1952 V6 4-door Ford Fairlane. I collectively purchased my very first pair of steel-toed Red Wing work boots, 3 pairs of denim coveralls, and a 10-pack of industrial-strength, rubber coated work gloves, as per instructions by my friend, Lee.

The next day, I was preparing to begin my first full-time job as a grave digger at Sunset Memorial Gardens on South Highway 81. Not something you'd possibly want to admit to someone you just started dating, but it paid well at $2 an hour. I could also assume that this experience would foster an adventure or two....or three. Well..,.that would be a gross understatement.

As I was driving south for my first day of training, I was thinking of different job descriptions or monikers that I could utilize to explain my terms of employment. I probably seemed more concerned about my reputation and ego than I did about payment compensation, which in turn would result in moving into my very first bachelor pad. "Yes, I'm a landscaper," which was essentially true. Or….."I'm a performing musician", which was half true, sort of. Or …."I'm digging graves while I write music and prepare myself for a career as a furniture maker. "That essentially made the most sense, but didn't understand how prophetic that would actually become.

As I pulled into the cemetery grounds, I was greeted by my friend Lee, and given a tour. What I didn't see coming, however, was a period of "initiation" which lasted about a week. Prior to that I was greeted by my boss, Scottie, a tough demanding old bird, and  Ambrose, who appeared right out of central casting for the "Beverly Hillbillies." I never saw Ambrose without his weathered smoking pipe between his chapped lips, which in turn, meant he was a man of few words. Last but certainly not least, I was introduced to Louie, (aka "digger"), a lifelong professional grave digger, who claimed he could recall the name of every soul he laid to rest. Louie was also profoundly full of bullshit, a toothless, hapless character you'd most likely see in a cartoon strip. His hands were like sandpaper, scarred and laced with callouses. Regardless, a kind, fallible, flawed individual. Probably miss him the most.

As I mentioned earlier….it was an exceptionally wet Spring, and the grounds were infinitely soaked, with standing water everywhere.

Burial interments were on hold, as pulling a 2-ton John Deere diesel-powered backhoe into position would greatly impair the surrounding turf. It was a delicate dance that the grounds crew had impressively mastered over the years. While waiting for drier

ground, bodies were stored in our "vault", in caskets of course, and in some rare circumstances, the graves were dug by hand ~ as with a shovel ~ which just so happened to be a portion of my "initiation". My first task was to stake out and dig a grave by hand, directly next to a spouse who had died a few years earlier. This was no fraternity prank, and the crew knew exactly what was in store for me. This was the real deal for an amateur "landscaper," an all day sucker, and then some. I will spare you most of the details, but my directive did include bailing water out of the grave using a coffee can. Use your imagination.

The "dreaded vault", as I called it, was a double doored, concrete-block, garage-like structure, originally built in the 50's when the cemetery opened for business. This was the most puzzling and disturbing cemetery policy discovery that was really hard to wrap my head around. This body storage policy didn't seem to phase the other ground crew members, or the management, for that matter, but it really seemed creepy to me and showed a level of disrespect to a grieving family. All this be-

"The vault"

ing said, during wet periods or extreme cold in the winter months, this is where we housed those precious souls for future burial. In a tiny unheated warehouse. It didn't seem very dignified to me, but it was the arrangement the cemetery had with the funeral homes. A padlock is what kept other folks out, except for the grounds crew, which now included me. The key hung on a rusty old nail in the shop and every time I walked past it I had to turn my head.

You see…..unfortunately, and my employment timing was obviously impeccably cruel, my grandfather was in that vault, as was my third grade teacher and a high school classmate who had taken his life. I couldn't shake the thought of seeing their faces and thinking how lonely it was inside this cold, dank, house of death. I understand there is nothing funny or pleasant about this….but this was my world, and by choice, my first full time job. Even today…..some 50 years later, it seems like a dream.

Eventually, my Grandfather, Carl Palmer Revland, was laid to rest, and I was proud and honored to facilitate that process. And before long, primarily using a shovel by all of us, the vault was empty. This "inaugural job" adventure lasted for about two years, and again, I won't bore you with hundreds of creepy tales from the dark side. Use your imagination, unless you prefer to close your eyes and imagine a coffeehouse performance I made three years later.

I will close with the chorus from one of my original tunes from 1974 titled "Everlasting grave diggin' blues".

"I've got them everlasting grave diggin' blues….
I've got mud stickn' thick to my shoes…..
I've got blisters on my hands for my dues….
I've got them everlasting grave diggin' blues."

Ironically…. 50 years later, I sit on the board of directors at Sunset Memorial Gardens, and the other board members "quiz" me on a regular basis. Most importantly…..the vault sits empty. What goes around comes around.

Chapter Twelve

NDSU Spring Blast Talent Show

1974

I t was March of 1974. I was two months shy of my 21st birthday, and my 2 year stint at the cemetery was in my rear view mirror. It assuredly wasn't a waste of my time, by any stretch of the imagination. It notably expedited my journey toward potential manhood, as well as granting me a front row seat to the "death in the family" experience. After burying more than 100 community souls, my mindset unquestionably switched gears, fostering the realization that we only get one, at times somewhat brief, bite of the apple and that the Funeral March was the ultimate "grand finale". I now realized that I could tip over on any given day, and that we are all granted a singular opportunity to get it right, and ideally, leave behind a legacy.

So there I sat.....writing tunes in our dilapidated 5 bedroom home on Third Avenue South, shared by four of my like-minded friends, all post teen social misfit stoners. Birds of a feather flock together. My only excuse would be that we were all products of the 60's. (Apologies not forthcoming). That being said, on any given day, a smoke ring could magically appear above the peak of our roof, as the proverbial "bong" was our tool of choice, and our delivery system. We affectionately called it our "Oboe" as it was crafted from a lengthy section of 2-inch PVC pipe. Enigmatically, we lived directly across the street from the AA clubhouse, something we considered relatively ironic, under the circumstances. We kept a running tab for every middle-fingered gesture that came our way,

One benefit from working at the cemetery was that it gave me an abundance of time to write some corny musical tunes.

- "Everlasting Grave Digging Blues"
- "Joe Dads Song
- "The Horses Run Around"
- "Alimony Honey"
- "Margaret's Song"
- "My House"
- "A New Life" ………..

were just a few, predominantly performed at our "kegger" parties at 1105, our $100-a-month homesteaded den of iniquity. As soon as I witnessed my legal age, I could expand my repertoire at our local pubs. Until then…..we live in the moment.

This night, however, was the piece de resistance, the signature dish, or in plain English, the real deal. It was the night for NDSU's annual "Spring Blast Talent Show", emceed by the legendary Ted Mack, host of CBS's Ted Mack Amateur Hour. I had been preparing for this for months, and had written an original song to unveil. "My House" was my ammunition, but I really had no visions of grandeur, and only hoped to create another adventurous episode for myself and my fortuitous friends.

I always kept my expectations low and within reason, but was also aware that the $100 grand prize would keep me in mac and cheese for at least a month. Customarily, we had a pre-party, as well as a post-party, for being identified as healthy, strapping young men of leisure, we invariably hoped that a bevy of young opposite sexed beauties would be in attendance.

The talent show event was being held at NDSU's historic "Festival Hall," one of the oldest buildings on campus, constructed in 1897 for $1,500. The list of performers there throughout the years had "Who's Who" credibility, especially from the "Big Band" era. Duke Ellington, Artie Shaw, Glenn Miller, and Benny Goodman had all graced the hall, in a building renowned for its tremendous acoustic value. Because of that alone, my exuberance was off the charts,

The performing contestants were told to arrive an hour early to meet Mr. Mack and do mic checks. Once there, the nerves kicked in, as did my OCD, and I started obsessing about having a brain freeze about the words and chords required to present my composition, even though I'd rehearsed it a hundred times. But who's counting?

All my friends were there for encouragement and by curtain time the place was filled to the gills, including the side balconies. Twelve performances, and I was the last to perform. Before me, and I'll never forget his name, was Scott Brandenburg, who tickled the ivories with one of his original tunes. After bearing witness to his offering, I actually was wishing I could sneak out the back door. But within minutes of hearing his thunderous applause, I was called to close out the night. Oh dear.

I recalled that my fingers were stiff and clammy as I sidled up to the microphone. I looked out at the humongous crowd of young people, heart racing, and plucked the song's intro on the strings of my Gibson 6 string guitar, hoping the instrument was still in tune. (Another obsession). As the first words of my song trickled off my lips, I suddenly felt at peace with myself, since the acoustics and sound system within the auditorium were beyond exceptional.....something fresh to me in all its newness. This was a life-altering moment for me, and I profoundly didn't want it to end, especially after the crowd stood and roared when

I finished the final Chorus. I clumsily bowed before heading offstage to join the others as we awaited our fate.

I don't think I'd ever felt so relaxed, just knowing this was finally behind me. Certainly not expecting to win, Ted Mack first announced the third place winner, who went on stage to collect her handshake and a $25 prize. Understanding the odds, I either won, took second, or was headed to a post party with my tail between my legs. I conveniently shifted closer to Scott, who I saw as the winner, after completing a performance comparable to Billy Joel. As soon as his name was called as the second place winner, I went numb. He quickly went on stage for his Ted Mack handshake and $50 prize, and graciously came backstage to root us on.

It was exceedingly intense backstage standing with the other 10 performers, none of which I knew personally. There wasn't much for eye contact, and you could hear a pin drop between us collectively, all anticipating the same result. Then.....the announcement came from Mr. Mack: "The winner of the 1974 Spring Blast Talent Show is......

I don't quite know how to explain how I felt at that moment.....walking on stage to a thunderous applause in front of my friends, while simultaneously wondering how I could possibly explain to them later how I didn't actually bribe the judges. All I knew was this was my moment to soak in, a giant bite off that previously mentioned apple, $100 richer, and an indelible fleeting moment with the incomparable Ted Mack.

And yes......there was a post party.

CHAPTER THIRTEEN

First Vinyl Record

1974

About 6 months had passed since winning the NDSU Spring Blast
Talent Show. It was September of 1974….and I was now of legal
chronological age, which allowed me the luxury of bringing my "man of
a thousand voices" act to local pubs and bars, one of which I had grown
quite fond of. However….saying I was partial to any such drinking es-
tablishment was a full blown misnomer, as I was beginning to enjoy a
variety of adult beverages.

The Kahler Motel Pub and
Grill had a very honorable crowd,
and respectfully refrained from
tossing ice cubes or chicken
nuggets in my direction while
I played, unlike my most recent
experience at Moorhead Senior
High School. I soon learned that
a younger crowd of teens would

The Kahler Motel Pub & Grill

not be as receptive, as being pelted with bus tokens while attempting Elton
John's "Goodbye Yellow Brick Road" would subsequently catch me off
guard. Perhaps they took more delight in humiliating me than catching a

ride home that day. Regardless….better offers were coming my way and I began to give credence to an assemblage of more mature human beings.

I had also recently been gigging at the local college coffee houses, quite enjoyably so…..as the audience leaned toward more of the female persuasion. This eventually, in turn, resulted in a consistent scheduled flow of Friday night pre and post performance parties at 1105, something my roommates were quite grateful for. Yes…..this was the seventies. If you weren't around, I offer my condolences.

It was now late September….and I had an appointment. This had been scheduled for a few weeks now, and I had no reasonable explanation for what I was about to experience. For on this day….I was cutting my first vinyl recording at Mark Custom Records in Moorhead. Unfortunately, I was battling influenza, complete with a fever, and knew I wasn't up to snuff. However, I obviously felt an obligation to work my way through it, as opportunities like this are few and far between.

I loaded my guitar case and a bag of cherry flavored lozenges into my 1972 yellow Volkswagen Super Beetle and weaved my way to the Moorhead side of the Red River. Sound engineer and local rock legend Bob Eveslage would guide me when I arrived. Bob was a member of the original "Unbelievable Uglies" rock and roll band, so I knew I was in good hands. Two original songs…..two hours, and we were done. I was on my way home to bed completely oblivious to how I sounded in that protected soundproof booth, or how many additional tracks Bob was adding. This certainly wasn't Abbey Road Studios. But today....it would suffice, as I ordered 500 vinyl 45's for my own pleasurable discretion and/or distribution.

The Unbelievable Uglies (1965)

About 5 miles to the south and west, final touches were being made on Fargo's first mega mall, a term foreign to most of us folks in the know. The developers, a local philanthropic family, would christen it as "West Acres." Within the confines of this multi-store outlet was "Musicland," where my friend John Cosgriff was working nights while he finished college. When my order of freshly pressed 45's arrived, a bumpy gravel road was the only thing that stood between my vinyl records and their potential distribution. I delivered a box of 50 to my friend John, hoping to sell a few copies at 99 cents apiece, which would net me half of that. The local radio stations were generously playing my recording, including KDSU, (the flagship station at NDSU), so by now, I was quite full of myself.

About a week passed since I dropped them off and I got a call from John one evening. He said, "You know Rev, sometime today you sold 13 copies of your

record, more than any top 40 record in the store." Well, after hearing this news, I was hopelessly beside myself. Visions of grandeur had precipitously crafted a nest inside my THC infested skull. We celebrated that night at 1105, home of the "bong", calling KDSU often to request either side of the newly sought after recording. We laughed uncontrollably, thinking the world was probably coming to an end. This was a long desired fait accompli, as I stated it was ok for me to just die the next day, if I wasn't so gullibly young, for soon I would come crashing down to planet earth.

I waited a couple of weeks to call Musicland again, as I wanted to soak up every glorious moment I had. Oh my......then the call itself came. It was Musicland, I'm sure asking for another box of 50. Instead....as my heart skipped a beat, they asked if I could pick up the remaining 37, as none had sold since that first haul of 13. They weren't selling. Really.

So.....much to my delight, or in this case, dismay, I soon realized that I had a fan club at my Alma mater: Fargo South High School. A small group of girls from the fan club, all 4H girls, made that trek on that bumpy gravel road, to dole out a hard earned dollar to support me financially. Touching.

Moral to this story: it's genuinely difficult to rid yourself of 450 vinyl records if you have only 25 friends. It would take decades for this purging process to come to fruition, leaving just a few in my own collection. Regardless, some yahoo in Ohio somehow came across one…thinking it had an extraordinary value of $84.96. If he only knew about the 4H girls. He should have called.

CHAPTER FOURTEEN

The Wood Shop

1976

It was February 4th, 1976…..a brutally frigid North Dakota winter day. Not the most ideal time to be asked to inaugurate NDSU's newest coffeehouse, the "Twenty After". After years of performing, and simultaneously honing my woodworking craft, I was not only feverishly preparing to give a knockout performance, I had also formulated the proclamation that I was unfortunately walking away.

I was uncertain how long this hiatus would be, so I decided that being vague about this announcement wouldn't be appropriate. But truly….. It was a "stick a fork in me moment". Through time, the thrill had considerably dissipated, and the stress attached to performing 30 songs a night was now unbearable. I felt I had left a mark, perhaps a small one, the magnitude of which was certainly up for debate. Still, I was praying for a good crowd, all the while knowing that John Denver was performing two miles away at the Fargo Civic Center. Oh my.

John Denver

Here I was, 3 months shy of my 23rd birthday and perhaps for the first time….deliberating philosophically as an adult. Once I was introduced and walked on stage, I was delightfully surprised at the large crowd of young people, as well as the number of close friends in attendance. I opened with one of my corny original tunes, but then spent little time delaying the inevitable, or beating around the bush. I don't ever recall being booed before, but the sound reverberated throughout the room like an echo chamber. What I came away with was a fortified confirmation that perhaps, I would be missed. John Denver I was not….there was no denying that. But this night was mine, and as it turned out, a life altering moment in time.

In between sets, I was greeted by friends, some surprised by my pronouncement, and others expressing some disappointment. Generally speaking though, everyone was supportive, yet inquisitive, wondering what would be in store for me. One soon-to-be new friend, was a slender fresh faced gentleman, generously mustachioed, and a year younger than I. He expressed an interest in getting together for a jam session, as his expertise happened to be the mouth organ, or simply put, he was harmonically inclined.

We met the next day at 1105, and music was actually never discussed, as he swiftly acknowledged one of my contemporary coffee tables in front of the couch. The conversation suddenly shifted to the fact that he, as well, was a furniture maker, and that perhaps we should consider opening a store. Well….one thing led to another and we

The Wood Shoppe.

soon opened the "Wood Shoppe" directly across the street from "Betty's Beer Depot", on the corner of 13th Avenue and 5th Street South. The location turned out to be advantageously serendipitous to both of us, as six packs were just a few steps away, and continuously achieving some level of utopia was a daily occurrence, as we hopelessly waited for the phone to ring.

Betty's Beer Depot.

We eventually took on a third partner, as the term "the blind leading the blind" required further acknowledgement. We soon acquired our first commission, an L-shaped counter/cabinet for Oak Manor Gas Station, so excitement filled the atmosphere. Weeks later, upon completion, which required a self help book (or two), we were informed that we had missed the deadline, compelling the owner to give us an "I need it by 5am or you can kiss my ass" proclamation.

We were up all night in preparation, and the sun was hovering above the eastern horizon. It was 5am and as we hoisted the cabinet to load it into the pickup, we were stunned to realize we couldn't get it out the front door of the shop. We looked at each other, trying to affix the blame on anyone....including Betty....and frantically got to work removing the 5x6 foot picture window from the front of our building. I'm quite confident by now we were each planning our exit strategy, as in how to withdraw from our verbal partnership agreement once this day was over. To amplify that perception, once we reached the gas station we realized that we couldn't get it through their front door as well. This exponentially became the last straw, an unmitigated coup de grace, and an embarrassment of riches. We were the keystone cops of the furniture making industry, and if we learned anything that day, we understood the need to measure doorways, including our own, before tackling any project.

Well....this was my professional woodworking debut. Not my proudest moment, but not a time to quit either. The three amigos, all flying by the seat of their pants, soon turned into two, and within a few months, it was one. I was now on my own, frighteningly so, and had much to learn. I soon carried a tape measure wherever I went. Lesson learned.

Chapter Fifteen

A Child is Born

1979–1980

The Holidays were again upon us in 1979. My furniture making business was consistently busy, even though I was still tutoring myself, as it was indeed a lifelong learning process. There were no cell phones or World Wide Web to amplify our life experience, so word of mouth advertising was the paragon of excellence. That being said…it was public relations that the majority of small businesses were relying on for success, and I was trying my best to implement that.

Tonight…..however, was a time to celebrate. It was a pre-Christmas Holiday Friday night, and I was planning my usual customary appearance at my favorite watering hole, the Old Broadway Bar and Grille. Disco was still in its heyday….

Gun cabinet (1979)

53

and I was an enthusiast, yet more legitimately, an amateur aficionado. I had turned 26 earlier in the year, and happened to be a healthy young man of leisure, enriched with advanced hormonal tendencies. Like many others my age, I was on the prowl.

I would consistently show up on these evenings donning a crisply-ironed and starched white button-down shirt with fresh denim blue jeans, invariably bottoming those off with my beloved leather penny loafers. By now, they had developed soles similar to bowling shoes, which worked remarkably well on the Old Broadway parquet dance floor. I also had a nice collection of sport coats..... probably 10 of them, which al-

The Old Broadway

ways garnished off my wardrobe, incessantly rotating them weekly. I had a precise method to my madness, which seemed to carry over from my daily studio chores, only that I was painfully shy....and always hoped I would be asked to dance, as that would be the only way to begin any conversation. There were many nights I would leave without muttering a word, but thankfully there were some ladies not as shy as yours truly.

Tonight was one of those nights. A great crowd, and the alcohol was flowing. I was asked to dance later in the evening, and we hit it off immediately. We spent the next week pretty much glued together, as I had shared with her my vast collection of adhesives in my workshop.

Within about a month, even though it seemed like just a few days, I was informed that I was about to be a father. Seriously. Due date: Early September 1980. We barely knew each other, but I soon met her parents, who were strict Catholics....something I was not. They also practiced teetotalism, a tradition that was never on my radar. Truth be told....and herein lies the rub, I, by now, was a hopeless drug addicted alcoholic. There. I said it.

Within time, the mother about to bear my child and her parents discovered who I really was, and refused to let me see her. I could not blame them......or her. It was what it was and they were only protecting their 21 year old daughter.

A few months had passed and I had pretty much given up on any form of reconciliation, until she showed up at my furniture shop, baby bump and all, expressing her love for me. I was utterly beside myself with optimistic glee. If the lights had been turned off, she would have glowed in the dark. Stunningly beautiful, yet preciously vulnerable. She had clearly gone against her parents wishes, acknowledging me as the father of her child. We were forcibly and undeniably immersed in a Romeo and Juliet moment, and we both had hungered for more familial support, only to get none.

I had now been invited and encouraged to attend Lamaze classes with her, as well as go on dates together, as we literally knew little to nothing about each other. I was confident I could overcome any substance abuse issues that were still quite prevalent, as this was the one thing preventing any potential future with her. The one beautiful thing we had in common was situated inside of her and I reassured her that whatever happened between us, I would see her through this pregnancy.

On September 3rd, 1980, mid-day, my phone would ring, informing me that the mother of my child was heading over to St. Ansgar's

Hospital in Moorhead. I quickly got my head screwed on properly and made my way to the birthing unit at the hospital. I found it unusual that the call had come from her mother, as her parents had basically abandoned her throughout her pregnancy. Having a child out of wedlock was too much for them to absorb I assumed…..until now.

Once there….I was quickly whisked into a waiting room, finding myself to be an unwanted third party. I was allowed to be in the room for the birth, but her parents were obviously now in their controlling, dominant jurisdiction. I wasn't good enough for their daughter, this was no surprise, and quite honestly, I understandably accepted it. Not remotely what we had bargained for though, and had us both feeling like teenagers. However……you reap what you sow…..and at the age of 27, my reputation was in competition with my future. Food for thought.

The next day, September 4th, 1980, Ryan Kelly Revland would come into this world filled with dubious distinction. A child without a father. A father prohibited from having any contact with his child or the mother that loved him. Within a month, they would all move to Wichita, Kansas. I was given one day's notice. A few months passed and I received a call soliciting a favor. "I'm getting married and my fiancé would like to adopt Ryan". I spontaneously agreed under all the circumstances that surrounded me, but under one condition that she verbally agreed upon. Ryan can contact me when he is old enough.

Stay tuned.

CHAPTER SIXTEEN

Mark Your Calendar

1982

This morning, I remained the consummate creature of habit, regardless of what may have crossed my path the last few years. I placed an order of bacon and eggs (over easy) at the Dutch Maid grille, my per-diem day break security blanket on Eighth Street and Main. This early morning emancipation was needed to facilitate enough momentum to round out my day. Familiar faces, sounds, and smells. The magic elixir blend for daily endorphin release.

It was May of 1982, and I was searching for a proper way to celebrate my 29th birthday, after spending most of the last two years in self-isolation. It was time to get on with my life. I had recently sold my two-bedroom bungalow in South Fargo to pursue a peri-

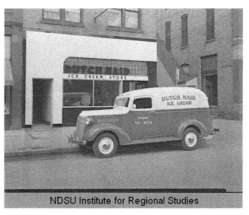
NDSU Institute for Regional Studies

od of simplification and downsizing. Renewal was the most logical motivational step toward moving forward, and basic sustenance was my new mantra. I was also cognizant that I needed to reintroduce myself to the community, make new friends, and expand my horizons.

Andreas and Issac Strinden, Shipbuilders from Strinden Hill, Städ, Norway, homesteaded in the Minnesota lake country shortly after the Civil War. Lacking a need for ships on the frontier, they hand hewed lumber into floors and furnishings for themselves and their neighbors.

Steve Revland, great-grandson of Issac Strinden, sculpts in wood in the tradition of his ancestors, with the same precision and fluidity of line that has distinguished Norwegian wood craft since the days of the Vikings.

Revland High Back Chair

In downsizing, and instituting an invigorating path toward evolution, I opened a new furniture making store three doors down from the Dutch Maid and simultaneously located an efficiency apartment directly across the street from my studio. That timing was astonishingly improbable, so I embraced this pocket size Eighth Street community as my new home, my belated birthday gift, and went out of my way to enter the lives of everyone that crossed my path.

I decided that 1982 would be the year of the "chair", my new obsession, something I had yet to tackle as a craftsman. The Revland "high back" soon came to fruition, as did the "Strinden Hill" foyer chair, both providing neurotransmitter stimulation, expediting my healing process.

Woodworking had become my natural antidepressant during the day, but unfortunately, drugs and alcohol continued to be a good portion of my evening ritual. It appeared to be a necessary

Revland Strinden Hill Sculptural Foyer Chair

evil, and it didn't help that the majority of my new friends were riding on that same bus.

The Old Broadway hadn't seen me for some time now, and the pub was now within perfect walking distance from our Eighth Street societal association, affectionately called "Top Floor". At least now I was attending with friends....conversationalists, much more comforting, which in turn led me to an introduction of perplexing magnitude. On this night....I was approached to be featured in a men's calendar called "Fantasies." Now....let's be real. I had yet to consider myself to be in that particular category, nor was I in any kind of "beefcake" physical condition.

The calendar promoters had wished for me to go shirtless, as in a bathing suit, so, knowing what would be revealed under my button down shirt and snazzy sport coat, I politely yet graciously declined. A day or two had passed and the calendar organizers by now realized that there weren't a plethora of bulked-up male patrons at the Old Broadway, nor other recruitment stations to choose from, so they again approached me to enter as a "fully clothed" participant. They even offered me my choice of month. Seeing as there would be no compensational offering, unless you'd consider massive ridicule some sort of stipend, I chose May,

my birthday month. They set me up for a photo shoot sitting on a century old concrete bridge piling on the bank of the Red River, near the offices of American Crystal Sugar.

After publication, offers for modeling came our way, and a few of us started doing ramp work, escorting, and of all things soliciting mockery, disco fashion shows. (Use your imagination). I was also asked to attend a woman's bridge club event one evening, wearing only a robe. The local modeling agency was getting quite audacious, in my opinion, and I always had the option to decline, which I did. Quite frankly, there was no reasonable explanation for exposing anything "flesh-like" to a group of 50ish upper-crust residents. Enough said.

Well…..the rest is history, and I don't have enough ink to explain what else was derived from this bizarre fortuitous experience in my life. It was however, in an outlandish sort of way, life-changing….. perhaps finding myself one step closer to maturity, as I was assuredly a late bloomer.

CHAPTER SEVENTEEN

California Dreamin

1988

Meeting "Elvira" at her California home wasn't exactly what I expected.....but I'm quite certain she was equally dismayed, anticipating an encounter with a blonde, full-blooded Norwegian woodworker from North Dakota, donning coveralls and a Cenex cap. On the other hand, for some absurd, far-fetched reason, I expected the door to open to the character "Elvira," in full wig and makeup, with a residence filled with Halloween-themed memorabilia.

No such luck. I expeditiously understood that the joke was on both of us, as we each knew I was there to take specifications for some tables I would be creating for her. The foreshadowing, however, was refreshingly hilarious and downright ice-breaking. As we shook hands, we simultaneously chuckled, as that handshake turned into a hug, like we somehow had been long-lost friends. That embrace somehow seemed naturally comfortable, and even congenial, because we each had a very close relationship with the incomparable Joe Cartwright. He was the catalyst behind a brilliantly conceived marketing concept, all courtesy of Joe.

Joe Cartwright was a native of Richfield, Minnesota, and a 1975 UND journalism graduate. We had lived together in the late 70's, and we partied together pretty hard between 1975 and 1980. Everyone who knew Joe never doubted how successful he would be, and to have this California connection would end up being a "be careful what you wish for" moment for me.

Joe Cartwright and Family

As our meeting progressed, I soon discovered that "Elvira" had a day job as a red headed meteorologist for KHJ channel 9 in Los Angeles. She had a high paying lucrative gig every year in October, for obvious reasons, and that extra income could afford her the luxury of acquiring some fine furnishings by a Scandinavian huckster craftsman from North Dakota. I was ceremoniously smitten in a "please pinch me" moment, and stored a plethora of humility in the pockets of my pants, only wishing I had worn coveralls to house the rest. She was more than gracious, and I wasn't remotely penalized for showing up in a sport coat with perfectly quaffed hair.

So here's the deal. Joe was sales manager at KHJ in Los Angeles and had access to celebrities, especially those that worked in television. When

Joe approached me about his plan to portray me as someone who had yet to leave the corral....I initially thought he was smoking fruit cake, until he explained to me that the majority of the West Coast population had never even heard of North Dakota. For these future clients to actually meet a Norwegian speaking, lefse consuming woodworker, would only add to their delight, offering them something other than sushi and authentic Mexican salsa. I would essentially become an acquired taste, if that makes any sense. It did to Joe and I placed my trust in him.

I would soon meet another (nameless) celebrity from ABC's Good Morning America program. She did the Hollywood Report for the show, and wanted one of my Signature Chairs, as she had seen one that I made for Joe.

Same situation.....same portrayal, different result. She was clearly perturbed by my outfit when we met. I was too slick and polished to be a woodworker, and she was unmistakably pissed at Joe for the misrepresentation. She wanted and expected to meet....the Other Guy. Our meeting was abbreviated, but still resulted in a chair sale. There was no hugging.

In one of my last brushes with stardom, in 1988, I was introduced to Steven (Rocky) Bauer, who co-starred with Al Pacino and Michelle

Pfeiffer in 1983's "Scarface". He was married to Melanie Griffith at the time, from 1981 to 1989, (sandwiched between her marriages to Don Johnson. He wanted me to build them a deck, which I had done for Joe's Hermosa Beach home, but at the time, wasn't in my wheelhouse. I can't deny, however, that while day-dreaming, I imagined sipping margaritas with Melanie by their pool. After all, I was still a young man of leisure, and had been granted license to theorize. Rocky's brother Victor Rivers, also an actor, threw the frisbee with me on Redondo Beach, another episode from my fairy tale existence. All this being said, if I could keep my shit together, this could go on for a while.

Steven (Rocky) Bauer   Melanie Griffith

For 5 years Joe and I expanded on this Alice in Wonderland undertaking. I would fly out every April and October, rent a car, and temporarily lodge at the Sea Sprite in Redondo. From there, I would meet clients, do some sketches, and return back to Fargo to fabricate items that would ship back to Southern California.

The financial reward was delectable, but so were the drugs and al-cohol. I was fearful this might soon be coming to a head, as the proof was in the pudding, and I was having more than my share of the gelato. Fruition however, is but a chapter away. Stay tuned,

CHAPTER EIGHTEEN

Paying the Piper

1991

I t was March 6th, 1991, a Wednesday morning, in the vicinity of 10 o'clock. The phone rang. I had yet to possess one of those fancy new cellular phone gadgets, as it appeared to be as substantial and cumbersome as a patio paver. You could actually take that new gadget with you wherever you went, which seemed almost unimaginable to me.

I, like many, was still enamored with the cordless phone, which I could literally take into my shop assembly room without losing any reception. However, phone reception was the least of my misgivings. And this day, as I approached my 38th birthday, my life was spiraling out of control.

Most days, I would leave my phone either off the hook, or in the "send to voicemail" mode….for the majority of my calls were coming from bill collectors or the IRS, as they had a lien against my home on Elm and South Terrace. Persistent drug and alcohol abuse had taken a hideous and disastrous toll….publicly, professionally, mentally, and physically. The Piper was now knocking on my front door, and the consumer in chief needed to consider letting him in for immediate, if not partial, payment.

Like I said earlier….the phone rang. Today, it was on the hook. Why, I'm not thoroughly certain. All I know is I was participating in my habitual, mid-morning daily exercise: smoking a joint and having a beer. I put the headset to my ear and cringed. On the other end all I heard was a faint whisper. "Dad?…..this is Ryan."

My first thought was that it was a prank or possibly a wrong number. It had been 10 years since I had attached myself to that paternal designation…..but the name Ryan admitting rang a bell. I paused for a moment to collect my thoughts. Thoughts that began to flood my mind with uncertainty. Could this really be my son? 10 years had passed since his stepdad had adopted him. I knew I needed to respond to him within reason, but also knew I wasn't in my right mind to adequately do so.

"Well hello Ryan. How are you?" I said. Anything else I heard jetted through my vacuous vessel of a skull like nothing was there, which at the time, sadly, was pretty accurate. All I remember was this: He was asking if he could visit me this upcoming summer, as his mom had promised him he could contact me when he turned 10, which today, Wednesday the 6th of March, he indeed was. And yes….he certainly did. Boy, did he. It was clearly a morning I never expected, or even dreamed of, but it turns out he indubitably saved my life.

As soon as I hung up the phone, I fell to my knees and uncontrollably cried like a baby. I was thoroughly and unquestionably broken. After gathering myself, I called my older brother, a psychologist in New York, and asked him to make some calls for me. Within an hour I was enrolled in an outpatient program at a local addiction facility. A humbling, but obligatory determination. The Piper was being indemnified. Paid in full.

My biggest fear....and I had many....was losing my mind without the mood-enhancing chem-
icals I was so accustomed to ingesting. Would my
creative juices shrivel up? Would I become socially
inept? Would I actually live beyond the age of 40?
[Something I had little hope of].

Fast forward 30 years.....

The rewards of sobriety are remarkably incalculable. Success is a daily multivitamin. My son, Ryan Kelly Oliver, now 40, is one of my best friends, and a chip off the old block as a musician, composer, and sound engineer. We were able to enjoy that visit 30 years earlier when he was 10. His mother.....(bless her heart) kept her promise: She let him call when he was ready, and that communication literally saved my life.

Take a bow Ryan.

Ryan Kelly Oliver / 2020 (40 years old)

CHAPTER NINETEEN

If Only for Today

1993

Living a few blocks from Fargo's Oak Grove Park certainly had its perks. Century-old towering oak trees, a frisbee golf course, and perfectly blacktopped walking trails…all surrounded by an expansive meandering bend in the Red River….certainly an ideal smorgasbord for someone pursuing a diet consisting of purposeful isolation, (like I did as a child 30 years earlier.) I needed no tee time to play a round of golf, and there were zero green fees. Just me and my $6 frisbee.

If the circumstances would ever present itself, I was what they called a "cheap date". But since I wasn't looking for such a thing, I wasn't about to hold my breath, and breathing was something I did plenty of. After two years of sobriety, I was still being awkwardly introduced to the world of manliness and a somewhat civilized society, all the while recognizing I was still emotionally trapped in my early

My classic driver.

20's, methodically lodged inside a 40 year old body. Ironically, the age I'd thought I'd never be witness to. How appropriate.

Oak Grove Frisbee Golf Links.

Today, as I artfully bend my plastic-coated flying disk between two trees to its intended target, I hungered for just a whiff of clarity and acceptance, as the majority of friends I had invested in for 20 years were gone, missing in action, like I was somehow contagious. I soon realized how few friends I really had, as being the former life-of-the-party and ringleader, I just wasn't fun anymore. Pretty sobering. At the same time…and I knew this to be gospel, I could potentially obtain, and deservedly so, my much aligned mojo, something I misplaced two years ago. I desperately yearned for my time-honored ancestral career as an artist, something that might take me into my golden years. This is really all I have, in a professional context, my one and only God-given skill. Frightening as this all seemed, I now take solace in the soothing sounds of morning doves, cumulus clouds, and pollen seeking bumble bees, all things I took for granted for years. I have for once located peace in the valley, and my soul has ultimately found it's rightful owner.

Back in 1987, I was fortunate to have the opportunity to purchase an old 1940 model flat-roofed mom-and-pop grocery store, on the corner of Elm and South Terrace in the Oak Grove neighborhood. I happened to pay more for my 1972 Volkswagen Beetle, so the funds derived from my California projects afforded me the luxury to complete this transaction.

Mom and Pop grocery store 1993

This had been my home for my furniture-making studio, but now, I was forced to carve out a 200 square foot section for an apartment, as my financial situation was untenable. Now….200 square feet might seem a bit tight…..which it was….but I was confident my current situation was provisional, as each day the future seemed a bit more illuminated.

To sum things up…..personally, I seemed to be making progress, through the help of Alcoholics Anonymous, often utilizing my new slogan "one day at a time." Seeing as I was living my life as a hermit, by choice, this slogan only seemed embedded into my own consciousness, as I don't actually

World's smallest apartment (1993).

recall professing it to anyone outside of AA. I was very private about my sobriety, never wanting to wear it on my sleeve, hoping someday to somehow magically emerge like the Wizard of Oz, when the curtain is ceremoniously drawn.

Professionally.....on the other hand, I was taking baby steps. I had finally proceeded to build a large china cabinet for some understanding friends from Grand Forks. For almost a year, the wood sat stagnantly in a pile, covered by a tarp, so I wouldn't have to look at it when I walked by. The stack of wood had become a symbolic reminder of my ineptitude and thorough disregard for uniformity. My twenty previous years as a craftsman appeared to be nothing more than a fraudulent illusion. I had little memory of any of it, as the entire dance was choreographed while I was under the influence of mood altering elements. But now....the tarp has come off, my mojo is returning, and my tools are again utilizing electricity. Quite frankly.....and it took awhile to wrap my head around this, I had come to one conclusion: For now....all I had was today.

"A million tomorrow's shall all pass away....'er I forget all the joy that is mine.....today.

Chapter Twenty

HGTV

1999

I t's the summer of 1996 and something called "Google" has been conceived. Not sure who came up with that ostentatious moniker, but that was comfortably above my pay grade. They christened it as a "search engine", which took me some time to wrap my skull around. But once I was able…..the expansive world of opportunity showed up at my door in the form of a personal computer, or pc.

Up until now, as a furniture maker, the choice of wood species available to me was limited to a selective number of lumber yards and saw mills, and if anyone is remotely acquainted with wood species native to North America,

California "Claro" walnut.

the term "pervasively boring" comes to mind. Most of my furniture made between 1973 and 1997 was made from Oak, Maple, Ash, Birch, or Cherry, all primarily sourced locally and regionally. Blasé to say the least, knowing what was on the horizon.

Most recently, I had discovered what was commonly known as the World Wide Web, courtesy of Google, and I couldn't seem to get enough of it. All I had to do was type in "wood for furniture making" into my computer and up would come hundreds of certified wood slab purveyors from Brazil, Mexico, and Costa Rica, not to mention California and Oregon, home to the highly figured and sought af-ter "Claro Walnut" species. Holy

Costa Rican monkeypod.

Moly. I was a kid in a candy store, with eyes the size of saucers. Huge, luscious slabs of wood, not just boards that must be glued together, had now entered my stratospheric curiosity. I could hardly sleep at night.

I now had the ability to purchase and manipulate massive multicol-ored, prolifically-grained slabs of Monkeypod, Mango, Parota, Prima

Olive wood from the Holy Land.

Vera, Santa Maria, and Acacia. Oh my....I could legitimately go on forever with the vast variety of exotic woods available to me now. The beauty of these tropical exot-ics was so breathtaking, I didn't know if I could ever go back to the mundane and monotonous local fare again.

I also was enthusiastically eager to create my own World Wide Web business site, as the potential to expose my wares to the world was aston-ishing and mind-boggling. What an invention! Whoever came up with this concept could reap millions.

The Revland "Signature Chair as featured on HGTV.

After showing my new art furniture at two local galleries, the "Art Connection" and "Nine Artists" gallery, my confidence level was currently at its pinnacle, and my desire to create art was pretty much all I thought about, which was exceedingly necessary and therapeutic. As I approached my 46th birthday, I was philosophically focused, calm and clear headed, and most importantly.....eight years sober.

The last few weeks, I had been preparing for a featured appearance on HGTV's "Modern Masters" program. I was one of four artists from North Dakota to appear on this weekly series, based on precise criteria, but not certain what that criteria was. Perhaps there was a specific doofus level required to participate, as this was something I assuredly specialized in. I would be featured creating the Revland "Signature Chair" as well as one of my latest designs, the "Enterprise" coffee table.....

all the while trying my best not to bestow embarrassment on the great city of Fargo.

In preparation for my appearance, because we only had 10 hours to film inside my studio, I needed to create three chairs in specific stages of completion.

The "Enterprise" coffee table.

In comparison, imagine a cooking show with Julia Child, where she first prepares a soufflé, but then takes another one out of the oven. Bon Appetit! With any luck, this could be a delightfully purposeful dance between man and an inanimate object. What a concept.

I tried my darndest to control myself during the taping, but I'm quite confident I scored a 9.8 on the doofus scale. The entire orchestration became a be-careful-what-you-wish-for moment, consisting of 10 stress-filled hours of filming, which was condensed down to a 10 minute nationally broadcast episode, just long enough to initiate the sale of 32 chairs once airing. I soon knew what I'd be waltzing with for the next 12 months. As Lawrence Welk would say: "Turn on the bubble machine". Oh my.

CHAPTER TWENTY-ONE

Fresh New Digs

2003

Turning 50, for some, might instantly signify a mid-life crisis. I absolutely and thoroughly understand. For me, personally, it was a marvelous and miraculous milestone, something 15 years earlier, as earlier speculated, I would have never ceremoniously celebrated. After 12 years of sobriety, I'm still attempting to catch up emotionally to my chronological age, but now having serious doubts of that ever occurring. I genuinely cherish the idea of being stuck at 39, as the late Jack Benny had a preference for. I hope that makes sense.

To commemorate 50 years on this magical, earthly planet, and with every intention of perpetuating 50 more, I perceived it was time to create some new digs. Consolidating mid-century modern living quarters with a detached state-of-the-art woodworking studio was perhaps my last "hurrah" so to speak….the ultimate utopian landing station for my amalgamated personal and professional life. What a joyful contemplation! However….I was also

Photo credit: Wikipedia

unmistakably aware that producing this "wonderland" over a one year hiatus, unassisted, would be beyond physically demanding, even for a 39 year old.

Once the strategic planning was formulated, my 50 by 150 foot property canvas was laid bare. I had a 1200 square foot shop space that would now become my "forever home" living quarters, and a 50 by 75 foot backyard that within a year's time, would be my little slice of Heaven, complete with a colorful courtyard and an updated woodworking studio. This more efficient studio space would continue to behave as my primary source of income, undeniably supporting my liberal leaning lifestyle, along with my coffee guzzling fixation…the one drug I've been granted permission to consume. All of this, all humbly so, in the historic Oak Grove neighborhood that I loved.

The main obstacle that I saw, if I chose to do all of the work myself, was my damaged rotator cuff. Thirty five years of full velocity tossing to first base from the left side of the infield had taken its toll. Softball was

Front side of finished home.
[Formerly Dan Luther Grocery Store. Built: 1940.]

certainly a blessing, but at the same time, a curse. I was aware that shoulder surgery was on the docket once my project was done, but at least I could rehabilitate in my newly-formed courtyard, knowing the work was behind me, all the while witnessing the resurrection of my multitude of perennial plantings, methodically interred prior to my surgical repair. August of 2004 was my goal for completion. We'll see how that goes.

Today was "pour the slab" day for my studio. I had laid 500 feet of hot water piping first, on top of 4 inches of pink board insulation, prior to the pour. Having in-floor heat is every woodworker's dream, as it makes furniture finishing a breeze, not having to deal with air movement within the confines. Seeing the finished slab on my backyard visual canvas only added fuel to this ambitious undertaking, which once the con-

crete had cured, was just a heartbeat away. I could also begin laying patio pavers…..25,000 of them….from my sidewalks to the alley, a formidable task indeed. My good friend Stanley Hoglund had provided me with these 4" x 8" colorful concrete nuggets, which in the end, would add color and texture to my finished canvas.

Framing the studio and finding a way to hang the roof trusses by my lonesome was, as one of my neighbors would eventually say,"Dumb and Dumber" in reference to a new Jim Carrey movie being released that I'd seen hilarious trailers of. I was a few months into this project, being September of 2003, and I'd taken a tumble off the roof a few times, fortunately without injury. I needed to "button up" the structure before the snow flies, so I could do interior work throughout the winter. I was keeping track of my weight loss throughout all of this, now standing at 20 pounds, which was a good thing, as I had multiple pairs of 32's folded and waiting to reappear around my waist again. Oh the madness of it all!

Fast forward to October 2004.

I missed my deadline by two months. Not surprising. And my shoulder was totally shot. The canvas, however, had been painted, signed, and delivered. I couldn't be happier with the results as I lay in my courtyard recliner, recovering from my much-needed rotator cuff surgery. It is a gorgeous Indian Summer day in Fargo, North Dakota, as I pray for a speedy recovery. I have a premium collection of wood slabs waiting for me in my new studio, so my mind is in design-mode overdrive, chomping at the bit to use some electricity again. I can't help but revert back to my childhood projects, some 40 years earlier, drawing remarkably similar parallels to today.

What a journey it has been. In actuality, nothing more than the journey of a simple man, trying to find his way in a complicated world. In a nutshell…..simply revland. Nothing more, nothing less.

Completed courtyard and studio.

CHAPTER TWENTY-TWO

Matrimonial Bliss

2005

The Spring of 2005 has sprung.....and our above average winter snowmelt begins its annual gravitational pull to its nearest low spot, creating the sweet sound of water trickling through curbside sewer grates. Like a babbling brook, if you listen closely enough, a significantly small commodity becomes a now more perceptive necessity. I somehow missed sweet nothings like this for decades, and now, after 14 years of sobriety, activity like this is music to my ears. Chirping chickadees, buzzing bees, and copious cloud formations.....all sights and sounds I perpetually took for granted.

Tonight....I have a date. Something in the 70's and 80's I had more than my share of, probably not deservedly so. I was a product of the 60's, Woodstock, Vietnam, Janis Joplin, and Jimmy Hendrix. All of which had a profound effect on me, and perhaps some not providing the best role modeling for a late-blooming young lad with an abundance of hormonal tendencies. I played hard.....too hard at times, scaring away many young ladies of virtue. Hearts were crushed, equally so, and I never seemed to cultivate solutions based on any reasonable interpretation.

Back to my date. Over the last 14 years, I can count on one hand how many dates I've had. Why? The reasons might show their manifestations on the other available hand. No bars, new friends, being overly particular, and having an independent streak a mile wide.

It was April 1st. [the day fools are made of] I wasn't the superstitious type, but I may have suggested we delay the date with Mary a week or so just to be safe. Mary's brother Bill, was a pastor and a good friend, and her protective family thought she was ready to date again after losing her husband in a tragic snowmobile accident a year earlier. She was shy.....but so was I.

We met at Bill and Pams for conversation and Trivial Pursuit. It didn't take me long to formulate that my personal pursuit was anything but trivial. I couldn't have been more serious. I had waited years for an opportunity to address itself in this way, and my fear of blowing it was showing up on my sleeve. I needed to decelerate, as this obviously presented itself as a marathon and not a sprint. She was sweet, quiet, reserved, and thoughtful. However, after reflective deliberation, If this was a ballgame......I think I was oh for four. What a doofus. I necessitated some diligence when it came to my social dexterity, and perhaps

after years of not being to the ballpark, I decided to cut myself some slack. I just hoped to get into the batter's box again soon.

It is now late May 2005, and I just acknowledged another birthday, number 52, with my new female friend. I really liked this gal, and hope she felt the same. I have consistently reminded her that being very low maintenance, all I needed was a litter box and a dish. I knew we were on solid ground when she laughed at my  substantially silly pleasantries, that being one of them.

A few weeks back, around Mothers Day, we shopped for annuals at our local nurseries, and equally harmonized the dirt-under-our-nails cavalcade, knowing that within weeks we could enjoy the fruits of our labor. As we serendipitously sipped coffee in the courtyard, perennial plantings interred in the Fall were also now making their debut. Shrubs, native grasses, ground covers.....all eye candy for those intrigued by such. Gardening and landscaping had always been a part of my repertoire, and I was digging it, literally, as was Mary.

 Now.....I would never evaluate a romance based on how substantial my tomatoes are. But Mary's plant food endorsement has pretty much tipped the scales. But let's be clear, tomato plants reaching 5 feet tall in 2 months could also be some sort of subliminal divine intervention. Not only can she increase the size of my tomatoes, she is kind, thoughtful, calm, loving, and attractive to boot. I have waited 52 years to get married. Perhaps I have met my match?

I have been having a formidable time balancing work and pleasure as of late, adding new digs, gardening, and romance to my carte du jour.

If only there were 30 hours in a day. I proposed to Mary last night....
with her four children in the room. I'm quite confident they are not
that thrilled with me, as a 3 month courtship may not be a sufficient
amount of time to secure a future with their mother. Also, filling the
loafers of their successful late father could also require utilizing an in-
dustrial strength shoe horn. But....I must be up to the task. Including
my own biological son, I now have 5 children on my imaginary magical
mystery tour.

Mary and I set a date for our
celebration of marriage: December 28th. But my father (Cletis)
had grown quite ill and we wanted him to be there, so we moved
up the date to September 24th,
which in hindsight, turned out to
be a Godsend.

I am so blessed to have met her,
as we can now provide tomatoes to
all of our friends and neighbors.
Life is good. Better than good.

CHAPTER TWENTY-THREE

Cletis Revland

1916–2005

Like all notions of dignity, fatherhood, in all its glory, inevitably invites the banana-peel slip of satire. A good example of this is the William Carlos Williams poem, "Dance Russe," where a father, allowed a moment of privacy as everyone else in the house sleeps, humorously dances in his underwear in front of a mirror, eventually concluding:

"Who shall say I'm not the happy genius of my household?

This is how I want to remember my father, Cletis Bernell Revland,

like me, another simple, silly, fearlessly uneducated man, who through sufficient schmoozing and a lovingly firm handshake, two stepped his way through the Great Depression, World War ll, and Typhoid Fever, something that just about took his life in 1946.

Here's an excellent example exhibiting the practice of purposeful parenting. As a child I once witnessed Cletis capture a fly in the cup of his hand through one full sweep. As he opened the door to let him fly away, He stated: "Flies don't have a tendency to live very long, so why cut it short. He may have a family to go home to."

Some household units have a tradition of wild game hunting, customarily handed down for generations. We didn't hunt. The determined extension of the life of the fly was all I needed to know. I have now become quite proficient at indoor fly catching, and I will let my friends do the hunting.

Cletis could also be quite clever when it came to teaching us life lessons. No spanking. No yelling. Just a pinch of mortifying humiliation would suffice. One day, when my brother was in high school, Dad found some condoms stashed in my brother's Converse All-Star high top sneakers. When Paul returned from school, we found Dad mowing the lawn. His choice

of landscaping footwear? Paul's Converse high tops. Nothing more was said. The message was clear and the guilt was delivered. All American style.

Paul and I discussed this. We don't think Dad gave a shit about the condoms. Edna, on the other hand, who at the time was Executive Director of a house for unwed young mothers, may have felt that some degree of shame should be proportionately administered.

Being a good and generous father is hard work, especially when you have 4 children, the youngest (yours truly) being a handful. Cletis truly understood my shortcomings growing up, resolutely exhibiting patience and empathy, yet at the same time, perpetually willing to play catch in the backyard, or giving me a nod while fashioning my seasonal projects. He was consistent in his consistency, and I felt that in my heart. Always.

Throughout my childhood, his love was ever present, and sometimes, as a father.....all you need to do is show up. If I only had a nickel for every ball game he attended, and there were more than a thousand during a 37 year softball career.

For every home run I hit, seeing his face light up, exposing his trademark thumbs-up, as I rounded third base. And for every image he took with his Minolta Maxxum 7000, as furniture progressively rolled out of my studio.

He also loved hearing me sing at funerals, as morbid as that may sound, but you see, Cletis was also a funeral singer for decades, and I took over for him in the early 90's, as his vocal cords wore thin. In fact, today......I sang at his funeral, trying my best to mimic his voice, as friends and family gathered at Bethlehem Lutheran Church, where he and Edna were charter members. He was 89 years old, lived a full life, and indoctrinated my soul with daily life lessons that I try to personally implement every single day.

Mary and I are so thankful that we moved up our wedding a few months so he could witness a miracle: His youngest, the black sheep who struggled mightily, actually found a soulmate. He passed away a day before our initial wedding date of December 28th, so it ended up being our miracle as well.

I sang his favorite, "In the Garden," at his service, the backyard location where Cletis found his summer solace. Generously, and notably, after all of my projects were done first. "First you raise kids, then you raise grass."

Heaven regularly welcomes award winning tomato growers. Rest In Peace Pops.

CHAPTER TWENTY-FOUR

Reinvention

2009

I've never lived in fear of the concept of reinvention. In fact, I have embraced it a number of times in my career and personal life. Reinvention is like skinny dipping. It is risqué and refreshing at the same time. It's periodically defined as a "mid-life crisis," which I've always found to be quite silly. Most artists that I know say there's no such thing. We..... being a small segment of society, mysteriously seem to age chronologically, but throughout a creative career, intermittently live our lives as a child. Admittedly, I certainly experienced a crisis, or two, or three.... It just presented itself early on in life.

Today, as I approach another reinvention, there appears to be a lot less drama in my life. At 56 years of age with 18 years of sobriety, one is authorized and expected to have his or her shit together. My dispensation has been properly established. My expectations however, continue to be somewhat tempered. I still have time, and time continues to be my friend.

Professionally, I can think of 3 major reinventions I have strategically implemented since the early 70's. In the outset, (the 70's), all of my furniture was fabricated from solid wood, which without proper knowledge of joinery techniques, you may be asking for trouble, which might include disturbing phone calls from folks. I received those calls….a cluster of them. Half of my time was spent correcting mistakes I had already made, the majority of which had to do with warping, cracking and joints coming apart. If your intentions are to become a furniture maker in North Dakota, good luck with that. Hot to cold, dry to humid, a recipe for failure without acquiring a boatload of knowledge. Truth be told, and there's no denying it, I was flying by the seat of my pants, without access to a safety net.

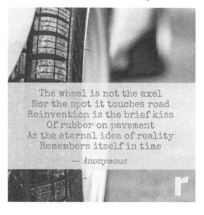

The wheel is not the axel
Nor the spot it touches road
Reinvention is the brief kiss
Of rubber on pavement
As the eternal idea of reality
Remembers itself in time
— *Anonymous*

In the mid-80's, desiring a more gratifying relationship with my phone, I converted to working with veneers. Much more forgiving, with a lower material cost. Over time, for better or worse, I milked that cow for 20 years, until my current resuscitation. The latest iteration includes the reintroduction to solid material. Over the last two decades, I am hoping that I have gleaned enough knowledge and expertise to make that conversion without much adversity.

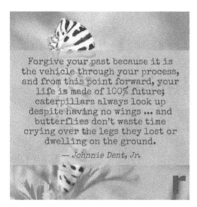

Forgive your past because it is the vehicle through your process, and from this point forward, your life is made of 100% future; caterpillars always look up despite having no wings ... and butterflies don't waste time crying over the legs they lost or dwelling on the ground.

— *Johnnie Dent, Jr.*

Going forward.....as I enter a new decade, my eyes are focused on abandoning the practice of designing and creating "custom" furniture for consumers. "What? Have you lost your mind?" declared my wife.

I had recently discovered something fresh and innovative called "social media", specifically a commodity called "Facebook". I had spent time researching how I could utilize this online entity, and the potential was quite remarkable.

Admittedly, I had grown weary of making multiple trips to homes, designing what would essentially become custom-made furnishings for folks. And through that process, these same folks possibly reject the cost of procurement. It happened.....unfortunately too often. If only I

could stock up on exotic material, design my own line of furniture, and sell it directly from my own gallery, or possibly through Facebook. How great would that be!

My conclusion is this: if reinvention is the mother of necessity..... adversity is the lubricating secret sauce. Stay tuned.

It is your reaction to adversity, not the adversity itself, that determines how your life's story will develop.

Chapter Twenty-Five

Revland Galleries

2012–2017

Negotiating with building owner Mr. Gil was no weinie roast. Originally from Winnipeg and of East Indian descent, Mr. Gil had the demeanor of the deplorable "Soup Nazi" from the Seinfeld sitcom. Whenever I frustratingly abandoned our negotiating booth from his restaurant in disgust, I expected him to yell out:

Photo: NBC

He was a disgustingly crude little man, loathed by the merchants up and down Broadway as a slumlord personified. I was warned to stay away from this creature, but the historic Syndicate Building was persistently in my crosshairs, and even if it took weeks to hammer out a deal, I felt I was up to the task.

Our negotiating meetings usually lasted about five minutes, and I'm quite confident I became a thorn in Mr. Gil's side. That, of course, was my game plan. He invariably, during each visit, tried to intimidate me, and when flustered, made consistent attempts to humiliate me. That's usually when I'd get up to leave, anticipating very little soup in return.

I would have certainly preferred dealing with a commercial real estate agent, but it was what it was, and Mr. Gil representing himself was the only thing that stood between me and my beloved Broadway location. Within time, after a dozen or so meetings of negotiation, I would inevitably open the "Uptown Art Gallery," kitty corner from the Ho Do, on the busiest corner of downtown Broadway,

Six months of renovation was now on my plate, and admittedly so, there were days that I questioned my judgment and lucidity. 30 pounds would eventually melt off of my midsection (again), a major renovation fringe benefit of necessity, and I'm quite certain this was the hardest I've ever worked in my life.

The Uptown Gallery (before).

Simultaneously.....I was recruiting artists to represent, and at the same time, I was creating funky fresh furniture to exhibit and sell. My wife, Mary, bless her heart, ascertained this adventure now coming to fruition, and although concerned, swiftly endorsed the concept. I had warned her three years earlier that when I turned 60, my plan was to open a gallery and sell my wares forthwith.

As I neared the grand opening, I experienced the same anxiety and excitement that I acknowledged as a child, as I unveiled my backyard projects to my neighborhood friends. This precarious escapade, on the other hand, was unquestionably more "adult-like" which would require a maturity level that I now felt was in my wheelhouse. Prior to opening, after a number of interviews, I hired Maren Day Woods to be my gallery director, a very wise decision for certain.

The Uptown Gallery (after)

It didn't take me long to achieve a stable of 40 reputable artists, local and regional, to grace the walls and floors of the gallery. And after 300 patrons attended the Grand Opening in September of 2013, I was a bit beside myself. I was unquestionably humbled that so many artists put their trust and faith in me. The community was receptive to another art gallery, especially in this choice downtown location. I was also fortunate that I negotiated an "out" with Mr. Gil, by paying for the renovation, which I did the majority of by myself. If all else failed, I could walk away, after improving his building, which had stood empty for ten years.

I spent my mornings creating art furniture pieces, and couldn't wait to hang out with Maren in the afternoon. The "Uptown" was such a heavenly place with folks entering with inquisitive saucer-like eyes, exhibiting their approval. We boasted a remarkable variety of two and three-dimensional works, so the gallery had a broad spectrum of color, texture, and shape. It was a good gig, and a community treasure.

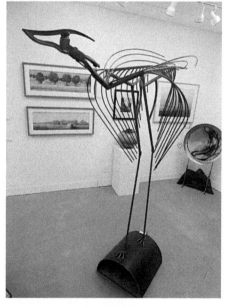

However....after three years, at $6000 a month, I took that aforementioned walk, and along with it, the knowledge and experience to open my first "Revland" Gallery and Event Center. Less space, less money, same agreement.

"I will improve the interior of your building, with the option to walk away when I see fit."

Revland Gallery

In both cases, the interior of these buildings was in such a state of disrepair, if I did take that walk, they'd have a leasable space and I'd be free to pursue other things. Essentially like "flipping" a commercial space, but utilizing it for my own pleasure after completion.

As I approached 2017, after a two year run at the "Revland," I was now presented with an opportunity that I couldn't resist, so I took another walk, each time gleaning valuable insight into how to run and manage an art gallery. 64 is right around the bend, and as the majority of my friends are now retiring, it appears that I'm just hitting my stride. Who knows....I might just be saying this 10 years from now. Stay tuned....

Chapter Twenty-Six

Dakota Fine Art Gallery

2018

I'm feeling quite nostalgic today, as I park my vehicle in front of 19 South Eighth Street. It's been a while since I've been in this neck of the woods, Fargo's oldest retail block, spared by the great fire of 1893. Almost 40 years ago, I had my furniture studio inside of number 19, appropriately named "Eighth Street Interiors." I also lived across the street in an efficiency apartment, so it was very handy and affordable. I desperately wanted to see what my old apartment looked like 39 years later, but I was late for an important meeting at the Mexican Village, a restaurant and landmark just a stone's throw away.....and home of the famed "Poco

Loco." I was pleasantly surprised to see my old friend Carol, still running the show at this famous ethnic haunt, something she has managed since 1975.

All this being said....my visit today was thoroughly void of anxiety but filled with a pitcher of comforting opulence. Today I was meeting with two of Fargo's finest artists and local cultural leaders.

Glassblower Jon Offutt
(+ yours truly)

Photographer
Meg Spielman Peldo

Glassblower Jon Offutt and photographer Meg Spielman Peldo

All three of us had been featured on HGTV at one time or another, so this is one thing we knew at the moment:

we were on a mission

...on this frigid North Dakota day, late February 2018, and it was about to get good.

After six years of gallery creation and sole ownership, I am now convinced that the only reliably infallible way to keep the doors of an art gallery open is to incorporate the cooperative business model. Utilized more consistently nationwide (and made popular by our local Gallery 4 for more than 45 years), they are the essential "proof is in the pudding" example of intelligent entrepreneurship. Seeing as the three of us have more than 120 years of practice between us, adding another 6 artists with similar credentials would be an impressive collection of local talent. This is essentially why we are meeting today. The timing is right, and the perfect location is conveniently available and within our grasp.

125 years ago, at 11 South Eighth Street, F Leland Watkins formed the Dakota Business College in one of the oldest commercial buildings in Fargo. Typing, shorthand, and accounting were part of the curriculum for thousands of students for more than 90 years in this architectural wonder.

And the three-story brick building still stands today, in all its glory. Watkin's grandson, F Leland Watkins lll, a personal friend for over 40 years, currently owns the building and has the main floor available for rent.

Lee, as he is affectionately known, is 82 years of age. As a trained architect (NDSU alum) over his long career, he has also been anonymously philanthropic when it comes to supporting Arts organizations. Unassuming and soft spoken is he, but very protective when it comes to the integrity of his prized historic structure. The main floor desperately required some TLC, but fortunately he has seen my other galleries and implies that he trusts that I (we) will create a gem….the main floor hub for the rest of his upper floor spaces.

One of my earliest recollections as a child, in the late 50's, was Edna and I being dropped off at the corner bus stop, on first avenue and eighth street, predicting that my nickel vanilla cone at the Dutch Maid was just a few steps away.

F Leland (Lee) Watkins III

If I had peered in the large front windows of the Dakota Business College as we walked directly to the north, I would have seen endless rows of students sitting at roll top desks preparing themselves for real world employment.

Today....however, 60 years later, I am able to gaze into those same windows, contemplating my creative offensive. I was comprehensively experiencing a "what goes around comes around" moment in time. Like I had access to

an imaginary time machine. This opportunity is something that could carry me into my golden years as an artist....and without giving it much consideration, I may already be there. Regardless.... It is my forgone conclusion and fortuitous intention, with the help of my partners, to create a world class gallery in a world class building for years to come.

After securing the 2,000 square foot space with Mr. Watkins, on a handshake, I created a scaled model of the new gallery space for his review. After accepting our plan, we went to work in the middle of March,

2018. We also secured 6 more members, bringing our total to 9, with a combined 320 years of practice between us. After our first board meeting we decided on a name. "Dakota Fine Art." We continued to proceed with anticipatory delight.

As I approached my 65th birthday on May 24th, I was also, to my wife's delectation, transitioning to Medicare. Oh my! How good could life actually get? The gallery is nearing completion, and my future health care is covered (just in case I step on a nail.) We are nearing the end of a three-month remodel and preparing for our celebratory Grand Opening!

On June 7th, 2018, my life dramatically changed. Simplistic motivational positivity has come to fruition. Our Grand Opening was a huge success with over 300 people crowded into our newly polished modern domain, as we served wine, food, and conversation.

The remarkably beautiful aspect however, was the position we put ourselves in, adopting the aforementioned cooperative business model. I won't bore you with the details, but we like to joke that we'd all need to simultaneously be hit by lightning for this to fail. Bottom line? Thanks to the philanthropic rental offer by our landlord, F Leland Watkins lll, this is here to stay.

In summary....I can now relax, stress-free, and spend my energy creating funky tables and chairs.

Did I mention my Medicare?

Medicare

Stay tuned to the final chapter (epilogue) of "simply revland."

> "I'm a great believer in luck, and I find the harder I work, the more I have of it."
> —*Thomas Jefferson*

Chapter Twenty-Seven

Epilogue

2021

Well....here we are. Present day, August 22nd, 2021. Chapter 27 of "simply revland" is in the books. It is a somewhat bittersweet moment for me, for as arduous as this has been, I've thoroughly enjoyed commemorating 68 years of an adventurous life. Escapades filled with discovery, joy and sorrow, and more importantly, recovery. I'm not precisely certain that I'd be alive today without committing to sobriety over 30 years ago. A somber narrative of a complex, troubled child, to a somewhat

problematic uneducated man, attempting to weave a meandering path for himself and anyone else who chose to believe in him.

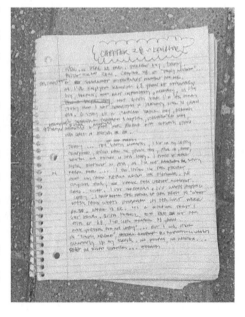

You all probably know more about me now than you perhaps wish you did, but it's too late now. That cow has left the barn. Probably the most difficult chore for me, through 27 autobiographical chapters, has been penmanship, and crafting

thoughts and memories into actual words and sentences.

I don't ever recall an English class that befriended, wel-
comed, or embraced me, but I
guess that's on me. Any authentic grammar lesson that I ever
received, considering I've yet to read an actual book, came from reading
the newspaper or listening to others speak. Ironically, two of my closest
friends today were my English teachers from more than 50 years ago,
each showing incredible generosity at the time, knowing full well I rarely
handed in an assignment. To all my friends, particularly English profes-
sors and bonafide journalists, I never met a comma I didn't like, so thank
you for your refrain and lack of admonishment.

Today on this hot, muggy, but
calm Sunday morning, I patiently sit in my lovely courtyard, pen in hand, wondering
how to write an epilogue to this
story. I somehow find it much
more difficult to pen, as I'm not
correctly formulated in a "mode
of reflection." I am living in the
moment, and anything futuris-
tic would be fictional, so I'm a
bit out of sorts. No crystal
ball….no "Carnac the Magnificent". Just today.

The late, great Johnny Carson aka Carnac the Magnificent.
Photo credit: Wikipedia.

However.....after some deliberation, it genuinely feels good, as it's a miracle that I'm even sitting here, quite frankly, and would give my left nut for another 30 years of memories to write about.

Going forward......on no given timetable, I will continue to blog about what's currently up my sleeve, the great community I live in, and how many rounds of golf I played. Woodworking tidbits will be served up and on the agenda, tables and chairs I'm tooling up in my studio, as well as any local cultural information I may be privy to. In other words, everyday knowledge that may or may not be of interest to you. You decide. No politics. No religion. Just good, old-fashioned Revland-enhanced bullshit. You can find my blog on my website, simplyrevland.art).

Now, as I continue to speak and write in present-day language, I want to thank my cousin Glory Hougham [huffum], all the way from Iowa. She helped me compile images and other information, and I'm sure, many times, wanted to reign me in, but seeing as this is an auto-biography, she affectionately got out of my way. I will always love and respect her for that.

In closing.....a heartfelt thank-you to all of you who have read my book. It has been a very cleansing and cathartic experience for me, and has brought me appreciably closer to my biological 41 year old son, as he now, like most of you, probably wishes he knew less about his old man.

From Revland's "Lake of the Woods" series

All this dirty laundry has now found its way through the spin cycle, and will soon be neatly folded and archived on a shelf next to the rest of my memorabilia. If this book has helped or inspired anyone at all, even one person, it has thoroughly been worth the effort. I guess I don't necessarily perceive this as a book about recovery, although it could be. I see it more as a testament that honors achievement and success, all through hard work and never giving up on yourself.

One last parting thought:

> 66 Forget yesterday. It has already
> forgotten you.
> Don't sweat tomorrow. You
> haven't even met.
> Instead, open your eyes and
> your heart to a truly, precious
> gift: today.
> -Steve Maraboli